THE LEFT IN FRANCE

the left
in
france

Towards the Socialist Republic

Edited by D.S. Bell and Eric Shaw

SPOKESMAN

First published in Great Britain in 1983
by Spokesman, Bertrand Russell House,
Gamble Street, Nottingham, NG7 4ET.

The Left in France
1. Socialist parties — France
1. Bell, D.S.   II. Shaw, Eric
324.244 '07' 09

ISBN 0 85124 349 5
ISBN 0 85124 350 9 Pbk

Printed by the Russell Press Ltd., Nottingham

Contents

Preface

This collection is intended to provide an introduction to the politics of the French Left for people who have an interest in French politics but who might not follow it from day to day with the attention they give to politics at home. We hope that readers of this book will get from it some idea of the structure, ideas and forces at work in the French Left and we have included a chapter on the new Socialist government's measures with an explanation of their place in the French political system so that readers can judge the importance of the French Left within the European tradition. Since we expect that many of the readers of this book will be members of the Labour Party we have paid especial attention to areas of interest paralleled in the Labour Party, hence the large sections on the internal working of the French Socialist Party and that Party's original Left wing — the CERES.

Not long ago many observers expressed gloomy thoughts about the possibilities of the Left's coming to power in France and even inside the Socialist Party there were those who doubted that they would ever win. Now France has a Socialist Government. We have tried to analyse the Socialist Party's sweeping success and have included some reflections on the measures being taken by the new government and the problem it faces.

It goes without saying that the sympathies of the editors of this book lie with the Socialist Party which we have been associated with for many years in both a formal capacity (in the Labour Party's Western Europe sub-committee) and informally through personal contacts. Thanks are therefore due to those who helped in the preparation of the book and to Ken Fleet for his encouragement. This book is dedicated to Roger Fajardie and J.M. Rosenfeld — great friends and socialist activists.

David S. Bell
Eric Shaw

Foreword

ELECTIONS AND PARTIES IN FRANCE

French politics has undergone a considerable change with the election of François Mitterrand as president in 1981 and then the election of a Socialist majority to the Assembly. The aim here is therefore to provide a brief guide to the politics of the French Left and this section will provide the background to the Socialist victories of 1981.

France is, of course, a presidential Republic. However the presidency is an institution which de Gaulle lifted to its current supreme position: the powers which the presidency has accumulated are not specifically given to it by the constitution. Despite the sovereign appearance of the presidency and the down-grading of the Assembly the power of the president in France is based on his ability to command a majority in the popularly elected Assembly chamber: for de Gaulle this meant the support of the Gaullist Party, for Giscard the UDF Party (plus the Gaullists) and for President Mitterrand this means the support of the Socialist Party. Like the Prime Minister in this country, the French president needs the support of the majority party in the Assembly and without that they are constitutionally almost powerless.

So if the presidency is the focus of political power in France it nevertheless remains the case that this institution depends on the Assembly and through that on the political parties. Without political party support in the Assembly and in the country the president would not have such an overwhelming position in current French politics. In this optic it is worth noting that the French Assembly has connived at its own lack of power: Deputies have been supreme in their opposition to the presidency not because of the president's threats or powers but because of their own lack of determination. This is expected to change during the next seven years and, indeed, has already started to do so. The new majority of the Left has made stands on numerous issues and compromises have been worked out with the government — this was not the practice of the Giscard years.

The Fifth Republic electoral system (which the new Socialist government wants to change) is a two ballot 'first-past-the-post' system. In single member constitutencies, if there is no candidate with an absolute majority on the first ballot, the candidates failing to secure 5 per cent of the vote are eliminated and there is a second round. Compromises and bargains can be made between ballots but no new candidate can enter the list. Very few candidates are elected on the first ballot and the effect of the second ballot is to encourage agreements, alliances, and bargains to take place inbetween rounds. The presidential election works in a similar way but with a run-off between only the two highest placed candidates on the first ballot.

The Left has always been dubious about de Gaulle's electoral system. Communists have constantly and bitterly opposed it as a system designed to work against them but Socialist opposition after their sweeping victory of 1981 may no longer be total.

The Fifth Republic has, until recently, been dominated by the parties of the Right and French political history of the last twenty-three years is the story of the re-building and re-grouping of the Left. During the 1970s France was divided into Left and Right and each of these camps was divided into two quarrelsome halves. Thus on the Right there were the Gaullists led by Jacques Chirac, the mayor of Paris in the *Rassemblement pour la République (RPR),* and Giscard d'Estaing's supporters grouped together into the *Union pour la démocratie Francaise (UDF)* which was in fact a coalition of numerous smaller parties who had more or less supported the Gaullists in the 1960s but never joined them.

This split in the Right was of paramount importance because it grew as Giscard's presidency proceeded. At present, with Giscard out of the political game for the time being, the two parties of the Right are of necessity somewhat reconciled in order to prevent their destruction by the Left. Gaullist Jacques Chirac is the major figure of the opposition although he is disliked by the UDF for having helped to sink their leader Giscard during the presidential elections (because of his attacks on the President) and by some Gaullists because he ditched the Gaullist candidate in 1974 in favour of Giscard. Chirac is a combative, abrasive, and totally dedicated politician but his record so far (except for a period as Prime Minister) is one of spectacular own goals. The future shape of the French Right is therefore somewhat uncertain and their truncated representation of 83 RPR and 61 UDF in the Assembly is not the most promising of bases from which to mount the counter attack.

On the Left the position is clearer: at the moment there is a large Socialist Party of 269 Deputies and a small Communist Party of 44 Deputies plus a few Socialist supported Left candidates. In an Assembly of 491 the Socialist Party has an absolute majority on its own and this makes Communist support superfluous although they do in fact support Pierre Mauroy's government in which they have four Ministers.

Since the shape of the French Left is the subject of the main part of this paper it is enough to note for now that the 1981 elections have brought to power a Socialist government with Communist participation based on an Assembly which is in place for five years and with Mitterrand as president for seven years. In the interim there are local elections in 1983 which will take an added significance with the increased decentralisation of power envisaged by the Defferre laws.

THE STRUCTURE OF THE BOOK

This book consists of three sections: One on the Socialist Party (PS), one on the Communist Party (PCF) and one on the major Left wing current within the Socialist Party, CERES. There is very little written in English at the present on CERES and as a current which has placed particular emphasis on workers' control it will probably be of particular interest to readers here. There is also an appendix on other sources on the French Left and a table of election results under the Fifth Republic.

Introduction

'A certain idea of France': the Fifth Republic has been dominated by the ideas of the coalition of the Right for the last twenty-three years, so much so, in fact that it came to seem impossible that the Right could ever lose power. Nevertheless the 1981 elections with their two Socialist victories have transformed French politics. Pierre Mauroy's government is faithful to quite another 'certain idea of France': the France outlined in Mitterrand's presidential programme in which social justice, human rights, are combined with technological progress to create a more humane society. Whether the new Socialist government can achieve its ends in a distinctly hostile international environment of continuing recession remains to be seen, but it cannot be doubted that the face of French politics has been irreversibly changed.

There were, in fact, very few people who would have predicted such a change in 1981: Giscard d'Estaing appeared set for another seven-year term. Part of the reason for this lay within the Left itself. Since 1974 the Communists and Socialists have not stopped quarrelling and, although there has been an armistice for the 'honeymoon' of the new Socialist government (which has Communist Ministers), the basic disagreement is still there.

However, the Left had thrown away the possibility of victory in 1978 by their quarrelling and as this continued through the presidential election of 1981 the Left seemed to have 'blown it' once again. Communist aggressiveness towards the Socialists did not abate and their talk of disruption, their racialist campaign and their histrionics seemed designed to turn away the floating votes from the Left and swing the elections behind the Right once again. Another aspect of this quarrel was the Communist determination to tar the Socialists and Mitterrand with the same brush as the Right: "they are all the same". (The discussion of the Socialist measures is to be found below at the end of Part I in Chapter 5).

Yet not only was there a quarrel on the Left between Socialist and Communist, there was also a quarrel *within* the Socialist Party. This appeared to be important during the years 1978-1980 because Michael Rocard challenged Mitterrand for the Socialist Presidential nomination and the Party was torn by this dispute. There was never any danger of a Socialist Party schism however because Rocard had said repeatedly that he would not contest the Socialist nomination if Mitterrand made clear his intention to stand. Eventually when Mitterrand did announce he would stand for nomination as the Socialist Party's candidate Rocard stood down and the Party united behind their candidate. Opinion polls had shown Rocard to be the most popular personality on the Left and had seemed to indicate that, whereas he could defeat Giscard d'Estaing, Mitterrand could not win. Thus the persistent quarrels inside the Left did not make it look as if 1981 would be a historic year for the Fifth Republic with the opposition moving into government.

However the quarrel between the parties of the Left probably masked significant long-term developments. For one thing the Left had become a 'majority' in France with the cantonal elections of 1975 and except for the short period over the 1978 elections there was a rising Left-wing move from which the Socialists principally benefited and which gave the Left victories in 1977 local elections in by-elections and polls.

Thus the Mitterrand/Rocard quarrel disguised this but it also became clear, as the 1981 elections progressed, that the Right was also bitterly divided. Giscard D'Estaing was vigorously attacked by his Gaullist 'ally' Jacques Chirac a fact which only served to underline that relations on the Right had been steadily deteriorating since 1976 when Chirac resigned as Prime Minister. If the Right was divided, Giscard himself made serious errors which contributed to the tepid support and hostility he found himself faced with in some traditionally Right wing areas. There were the scandals (the truth of which may never be really known) and a certain insensitivity (on foreign policy for example) to his own electorate which meant that the extremely narrow margin of Giscard's 1974 victory did not look likely to be increased and, of course, unemployment and inflation did not seem to be under control. Giscard probably lost due to a combination of these factors. These, however, are the negative reasons for the Right's loss of 'their' institutions and the movement of the Socialists into power. To the positive account must be put the desire for change after twenty-three years of Right-wing rule and the excellent campaign run by François Mitterrand around the theme of the 'tranquil force' which managed to win over the margin of floating voters which had been missing in 1974 but which moved over to the Left in 1981. The Socialist Party swept to a majority in the Assembly on the coat-tails of the Mitterrand victory and supporting the '110 propositions' which had featured in the presidential campaign and they faced a demoralised and divided Right which gave no real opposition; hence the so-called 'state of grace' (in American presidential parlance 'honeymoon period') after the elections which ran into the autumn of 1981.

The first chapter of this part deals with the history of French Socialism up to the election victory of 1981, chapter two deals with the sociology of the Socialist Party (its voters, activists and supporters), chapters three, four and five deal with the organisation of the Socialist Party and with what the Party is going now that it has taken power and it looks at the government programme in some detail.

CHAPTER ONE

The Evolution of French Socialism

by David S. Bell and Eric Shaw

THE SFIO 1920-1970

Periods of unity on the French Left are brief interludes brightening up a history of dissension and acrimony. In France there has been a single party of the Left only for a brief spell of fifteen years — from 1905 to 1920. In 1905 the leaders of the Second International persuaded the rival socialist parties of Jean Jaures and Jules Guesde to bury their differences and form a single party — called, in recognition of the role played by the International, the SFIO: The French Section of the Workers' International.

Unity lasted only until 1920. At the Congress at Tours in that year, the SFIO debated whether to affiliate to the Communist International. A majority of delegates were in favour, and proceeded to form the French Communist Party (PCF). A minority strongly resented the move and re-established the SFIO. Henceforth, except for short and transitory periods, the two parties were to be bitter foes. In the early years (the 1920s and the early 1930s) each party struggled for ascendency on the Left. Their relations were often venomous and a pattern of mutual distrust and animosity was set which was to complicate all future efforts at co-operation.

Initially, it was the SFIO which survived the schism in better shape. Membership expanded, voters flocked in large numbers to the Party and within a few years it easily outpaced the Communists in size and influence. In addition, the main train union federation, the CGT, was better disposed to it than the Communists. It was the premier force on the Left — a position it was to hold for all too short a time.

In 1934, Stalin reversed his earlier policy and ordered the members of the Communist International to mend fences with the Social Democratic parties (until then fiercely assailed as 'social fascists') and seek to form 'Popular Fronts' with all democratic and progressive elements. It was a belated recognition of the Nazi menace which had already destroyed the large Communist and Social Democratic parties in Germany with equal impunity.

The SFIO responded to Communist overtures and an alliance was formed between the Socialist, Communist and Radical parties, known and still celebrated as the Popular Front. The Front was swept to power in the elections of 1936 and Léon Blum, the SFIO leader, became the first Socialist Prime Minister in France.

The Popular Front government provided the first instance of Socialist-Communist co-operation, but it had a short and troubled history. It aroused tremendous enthusiasm, and a number of notable reforms were enacted. However, the Communists refused to accept ministerial posts, and the government was riven by disputes between Socialists and Radicals. It survived only until 1938, when the Radicals deserted to form a coalition with right-wing groups.

In 1939, the Nazi-Soviet Pact was signed, and the PCF fell dutifully into line. Enmity between the two parties of the Left flared up anew. However, the Communists restored their prestige on the Left after 1941 (when Hitler attacked the Soviet Union) by the energetic part they played in the Resistance. Communists and Socialists (and Catholics) fought side by side against the German occupiers and the Vichy authorities, and Left-wing unity once more proved attainable. So, with the end of the war, many ardently hoped that wartime co-operation would carry forward into peacetime.

These hopes were initially realised. The immediate post-war period witnessed the second (and again brief) instance of Socialist-Communist collaboration. In the elections of 1945, the Left won an absolute majority — with the Socialists reaching their highest vote yet and the Communists performing even better to become the largest party in France. The two parties combined with the newly-founded Christian Democratic Party (the MRP) to form a government: the so-called era of *tripartisme.*

Again, unity was not to endure for long. The international

climate soon darkened. By 1947, all pretence at harmony between the wartime allies (the United States, Soviet Union and Britain) was dropped and the glacial age of the Cold War commenced. This had repercussions throughout Europe. In the Eastern half of the continent, the Soviet grip tightened ever more firmly, and countries within Moscow's sphere of influence were reduced to satellite status. In the West, the Americans used their considerable economic and political influence to secure the eviction from office of Communist ministers in France and Italy.

By this time, relations between the PCF and SFIO had deteriorated again, and the latter willingly formed coalitions with the MRP and Radicals. These centrist coalitions were dubbed the 'third force' as they contended with Communists on the Left and Gaullists and others on the Right.

The Fourth Republic had been established in 1946. It lasted for twelve years — years which were disastrous for the SFIO. With democracy endangered by authoritarians on Right and Left, it felt it had no alternative but to participate in governing with the centre and moderate Right. Unity on the Left (a prerequisite for a Left government) seemed precluded by the Stalinist character of the PCF, and its obsequious subordination to Moscow.

Yet, if the circumstances were admittedly difficult, it is hard not to conclude that the SFIO made them even worse. Under the leadership of Guy Mollet — elected as General Secretary in 1946 and destined to retain that post over two decades — the Party contrived a peculiarly unappealing combination of Marxist rhetoric and visionless pragmatism. Officially spurning reformism in favour of the class struggle, the SFIO proved unwilling to push or incapable of securing the implementation of progressive economic and social legislation. Both in terms of organisation and policy, the arteries of the Party visibly hardened. Membership dwindled, support continuously declined throughout the country and growing numbers of critics left the Party in total disillusion.

For many, the conduct of the Socialist-led government of 1956 was the final straw. After participating enthusiastically in the disastrous Suez expedition, Guy Mollet, the Prime Minister, reversed Socialist policy over Algieria, throwing the weight of the government full square behind the settlers and the local military authorities, hence signalling his preference for a strategy of repression rather than negotiation with the Algerian muslim guerrilla forces. The gap between actions and words became so wide that, by the time the Fourth Republic expired in 1958, the SFIO was thoroughly discredited.

Initially, the SFIO backed the new government of General de Gaulle (though a substantial minority dissented) but moved into opposition as the determination of the General to effect major alterations in the political structure of the country became clearer. The Republic of the parties was over. Parliament was denuded of many of its powers, and the political forces most closely identified with the unpopular Fourth Republic fell into gradual decay. By the 1960s, the SFIO realised that its stay in the political wilderness might well be protracted.

Not that its leaders saw this as any cause to contemplate a profound revaluation of the Party's organisation, policies or strategy. Their initial response was to concentrate on forging electoral alliances which might allow a speedy return to the corridors of power (or, more accurately, office). But if the Party stayed the same, the environment in which it lived was changing rapidly, and irreversibly.

The nature of the change was three-fold — economic, social and institutional, of which the first was, in many ways, the most striking. The rate of economic growth, which for years had lagged behind that of most of her neighbours, spurted. By the 1960s, France had emerged as one of the West's leading industrial powers. Whereas, not so long before, the country had been best known for her wine and food, by the 1960s, the typical French product was the motor-car. The long, delayed process of industrialisation was now completed. By 1975, industry accounted for 37.2 per cent of GPD.

The nature and size of the typical French firm also altered very considerably. Partly in response to market conditions, partly due to direct government encouragement, a wave of amalgamations and take-overs transformed the structure of French industry. Nowadays, the average French worker (manual or white collar) is employed by a large firm, state or privately-owned, and an increasing proportion by multinational firms.

Economic growth and centralisation have inevitably changed the composition of the labour-force. The percentage of peasants and farmers has fallen from 20.9 per cent in 1954 to 7.6 per cent in 1975. The numbers of employers and the self-employed in commercial and industrial pursuits has also undergone a significant decline. In the same period the porportion of manual workers rose slightly from 33.8 per cent to 37.2 per cent, while that of white collar workers grew very rapidly from 16.8 per cent to 30.3 per cent.[1] These shifts in the social structure had potentially significant consequences for two reasons.

Firstly, the fall in the number of employers and self-employed is weakening considerably a natural constituency of the Right. Secondly, the social stratum which has experienced the most rapid expansion — white collar workers — is one whose political loyalties are traditionally indeterminate and divided. Clearly, any political party which gained the loyalties of large numbers of white collar workers would flourish electorally.

The final type of change was institutional. The establishment of the Fifth Republic led to major modifications in the French political system. Briefly, these were, first, the creation of a powerful executive with an increasingly influential president elected, after a constitutional amendment in 1962, by popular vote. Secondly, a marked diminution in the powers of Parliament. The French National Assembly was divested of so many powers that from being one of the most influential legislatures in the Western world it was reduced to the status of one of the least powerful. This, inevitably, substantially lessened the direct importance of the political parties, in particular those straddling the centre of the political spectrum, who dominated governments under the Fourth Replublic — the SFIO, Radical and the MRP (Christian Democrats). Finally the electoral system changed to a single-constituency, double-ballot procedure which greatly favoured the largest party, or the most cohesive political bloc.

Related to these constitutional and institutional changes was the rapid rise to ascendancy of the Gaullist Party whose

main function, in the 1960s and early 1970s, was to provide
steadfast support for President de Gaulle and his Gaullist
successor, President Pompidou. The installation of a
Presidential system, and the dominance of the Gaullists had a
pervasive impact on the whole political scene. Contests for
the Presidency — the key political institution of Fifth
Republic France — by their very nature encourage the
formation of majoritarian political formations i.e. blocs
which can gain more than 50 per cent of the popular vote.
Under the Fourth Republic, parties neither sought nor could
realistically aspire to gaining outright majorities at elections.
At best, they could add a few percentage points to their
totals, improving their bargaining power in the negotiation
over the forming of the next government. This was no longer
adequate. Insofar as executive power was concentrated in the
Presidency, political forces which strove for it must build up
a coalition around a presidential candidate who could attract
the support of a majority of the electorate.

In the case of de Gaulle, his ascent to the Presidency
preceded the creation of a majoritarian political party. But
he, and his advisors, saw the need for such a party if he was
to retain a firm grip on both the Presidency and also the
National Assembly, where majority support was still vital.

Unlike in Britain, the Right in France before 1958 has
never been organised in a single, united and disciplined party,
with a wide-ranging popular appeal. The emergence of a
powerful Gaullist Party was therefore an event of decisive
political importance. In a series of electoral triumphs in the
early 1960s, the Gaullists swept all before them. They
gradually absorbed most of the traditional, ill-organised
parties of the Right — with some exceptions like Giscard
D'Estaing's Independent Republicans who were, however,
closely allied with the Gaullists for most of the period. In the
late 1960s, President Pompidou turned his attention to the
centre parties and they, too, (apart from the Left wing
Radicals, the MRG) were successfully wooed into alliance
with the Gaullists and inclusion in the government.

The various developments outlined above suggested that
the SFIO's eviction from government might not be temporary
as its leaders first supposed. However, it took several years
before the Party began seriously to consider the implications

of these developments, years when it became ever more evident that its return to government would be neither swift nor easy. The SFIO's first response was tactical and electoral in character: namely, by what means could it muster sufficient strength to challenge the supremacy of the newly united conservative forces? Since, clearly, its own resources were insufficient, suitable partners had to be discovered.

There were two possible options for the Party: incorporation into a grand alliance or federation of the centre and moderate Left, or alliance with the Communists. The two were not, in fact, mutually exclusive. Proponents of the first believed that the creation of a strong federation of the centre-Left would permit negotiations with the Communists on terms of equality. The supporters of the latter aimed to rebuild a strong party of the moderate Left after an alliance with the Communists had been agreed.

In those far-off days of the early 1960s when 'old-fashioned socialism' appeared a discredited doctrine the model of all middle of the road progressives was John Kennedy's Democratic Party. Undoubtedly this model helped to inspire Gaston Defferre, Socialist Mayor of Marseilles and leading advocate of the centre-Left formula.

Defferre was the head of the SFIO federation of the Bouches-du-Rhône, one of the big three working class federations of the post-war SFIO. (The other two were Augustin Laurent's Nord and Guy Mollet's Pas-de-Calais). In Marseilles, Defferre had revived a moribund and divided SFIO into the dominant political force in the city by uniting the reformist centre-Catholics and liberals — around a Socialist Party which provided the driving force in city politics. Defferre's ambition was to repeat this success on the national stage.

His aim was to present himself as the candidate of a democratic and progressive alliance in the 1965 Presidential election. To that end he engaged in laborious and protracted negotiations with all the potential constituents of such an alliance — his own SFIO, the MRP, the Radicals, and the non-affiliated political clubs which were mushrooming in this period.

The scheme failed. Many within his own party (including the General Secretary, Guy Mollet) were either lukewarm or hostile. Similarly, the Catholic MRP entertained many reservations. Undermined from within the SFIO, unable to secure the full-hearted co-operation of the other political groups, a disheartened Defferre eventually gave up.

Unlike many SFIO politicians, Defferre had a clear and coherent notion of the type of party he wanted. It would have no truck with the hypocricies of the SFIO — the yawning gap between professed ideals and actual behaviour, the clinging dogma which alienated potential allies but was totally disregarded in practice; it would cease pretending that it sought to transform French society, but would be content with a solid programme of social reforms; it would be pragmatic, enlightened and technocratic in outlook. In short Defferre's project was one Hugh Gaitskill would have understood and commended.

After the Defferre strategy collapsed the SFIO was left with the second option: some kind of arrangement with the Communists. At this point, François Mitterrand stepped into the limelight. Mitterrand had been a member of a small centre-Left group of notables (the UDSR) in the Fourth Republic. He had participated in a number of governments of varied political complexion. He had several advantages which aided his emergence as the major figure on the non-Communist Left. He did not belong to a major political party — and had therefore made fewer enemies than Defferre; he had been identified with no controversial causes and appeared to have no strong principles. In short he was a rather neutral character who rose to prominence not because many supported him but because few objected to him. Unlike so many others in the Centre and Left, he could not be charged with betraying his ideals because he had never averred his allegiance to any.

Mitterrand managed to cobble together a 'mini-federation' consisting of the SFIO, the Radical and his own supporters organised in the CIR club (Convention of Republican Institutions). This was known as the Federation of the Left (FGDS). It was ready after the 1965 Presidential election. Mitterrand also secured the crucial backing of the Communists. He performed well at the polls, forcing de Gaulle to a second ballot, and earning himself considerable prestige. He then sought to build up the Federation, and move towards a closer relationship with the Communists. Everything appeared to go smoothly. The FGDS and the PCF signed an electoral agreement in time for the 1967 legislative elections, when both made useful gains. Steps were even taken towards producing a joint statement of policy objectives which was done in early 1968.

But 1968 destroyed all this work. The combination of the May 'events', the Left's total rout in the subsequent elections, and the Soviet invasion of Czechoslovakia the following August led to a sharp deterioration of relations with the Communist Party, followed by the disintegration of the Federation of the Left. Mitterrand also discredited himself in a rather mis-timed announcement that he was ready to present himself as a candidate for the presidency during the 1968 'events'.

In the Presidential elections of 1969, the Socialists sank to their lowest level. The Left failed to agree on a common candidate. Instead three men entered the race under Left-wing colours — the Communist Jacques Duclos, Defferre on behalf of the Socialists and the PSU leader Michel Rocard. Duclos captured a bit more than the regular Communist 20 per cent of the vote, whilst Defferre attracted a derisory 5 per cent which compared badly with Rocard's 3½ per cent, an impressive figure for a representative of a minor party of the Left with minute Parliamentary representation.

Veteran statesmen, it is sometimes said, die shortly after retirement because, having been rendered politically superfluous, they lose the will to live. This sums up the fate of the SFIO in 1969. Its political bankruptcy was there for all to see. Having tried one expediency after another, it had failed to reverse its steady decay. In 1969 it decided to disband.

"Le roi est mort. Vive le roi!" A change of name — in 1969 it became the Socialist Party (PS) — a new General Secretary (Alain Savary), and phoenix-like, it was hoped, a new dynamic party would rise from the ashes, though the same men (like Guy Mollet) were pulling the strings. In 1969, however, this manoeuvre failed to carry conviction. Savary put in hard work and stemmed the decline of the non-Socialist Left's main Party but he had neither the backing nor the stature (needed to provide a presidential focus) to start a real renewal. The only person capable of this feat was

Mitterrand who was still outside the Party. Accordingly a fusion of various groups to bring him to the leadership of the PS was arranged. Thus the real rebirth of the Party took place at Epinay two years later, in 1971. Present at the fusion were SFIO stalwarts, representatives of Left Wing political groups, François Mitterrand's own political club (the CIR), CERES, the Left-wing ginger group within the SFIO, and various independents. This time, the old guard was overthrown, and Mitterrand, having manoeuvred to join the Socialist Party, was duly installed as First Secretary.

THE SOCIALIST PARTY 1971-1982

The coalition of groups which secured the leadership for Mitterrand was a rather unlikely one, comprising the new First Secretary's CIR, one section of the old SFIO establishment led by Defferre and Mauroy (boss of the Socialist stronghold of the Nord) and CERES, the Party's *suiviste* Marxist wing. These three currents, after 1971, controlled the new Party, occupying all the positions in the Secretariat. Despite their various differences of view, they had sufficient in common to enable the PS to embark on a more or less coherent strategy. This consisted of two major elements: firstly the revitalisation of Party organisation and policy around Mitterrand, and, secondly, the creation of a working alliance with the Communists around a joint manifesto — the Common Programme.

Rapid progress was made on both fronts, Party organisation was revamped, and membership grew rapidly. A considerable amount of energy was devoted to rethinking Party policy. Particular prominence was given to the policy of *autogestion* (self-management) in all spheres of social, economic and political life — indeed it became one of the identifying characteristics of the new Socialist Party. As far as the second major element — relations with the Communists — was concerned, in June 1972, within a year of Mitterrand's takeover a Common Programme of Government had been signed. The Common Programme consisted of a set of legislative proposals which a Left-wing government would enact in its first term of office, together with an effort to reconcile the two parties on issues which traditionally divided Socialists and Communists. Then followed a period of honeymoon which lasted until September 1974 when marital difficulties set in. These eventually culminated in divorce (or, at least, separation) in the autumn of 1977.

At first, however, all was well. A year after the Common Programme was signed, the new Union of the Left faced its first test — the legislative elections of 1973. Socialists and Communists co-operated well and although the Right emerged triumphant, both parties of the Left made useful advances.

In 1974 President Pompidou unexpectedly died. It was agreed, without any difficulty, to field Mitterrand as the candidate of the united Left. In contrast to the presidential election of 1965, it was the Left which on the first ballot, rallied behind a common candidate whilst the Right, split between the Gaullist Chaban-Delmas and Giscard D'Estaing, was in considerable disarray. Noticeably, during the campaign, Mitterrand distanced himself from the Common Programme (he hardly mentioned it) and softened the contours of Left-wing policy. The Communists behaved in a rather self-effacing way, refraining from any pronounce-ments and activities which could embarrass Mitterrand, making no effort to tie him down to the Common Programme, but using the Party apparatus to support him.

Mitterrand lost by the narrowest of margins (around 1 per cent of the total vote cast on the second ballot). Although the Socialists were naturally somewhat disappointed they were also considerably heartened by the evidence of an upsurge in electoral popularity. Priority was once more given to building up the Party.

Within a few months of the 1974 elections, the PS received a new influx of recruits. Led by Michel Rocard, a former leader of the PSU and presidential candidate in 1969, a minority seceded from the Far Left PSU and joined the Socialist Party. An attempt to secure the adhesion of the Leftist Trade Union Federation the CFDT, however, failed.

The arrival of Rocard and his followers caused some problems. Both Rocard and the PSU (which had refused to sign the Common Programme in 1972) were greatly distrusted by the Communists. The latter, already disturbed by by-election results which showed continued progress for the Socialists but a decline in their own popularity, sharpened their criticisms of the PS.

Inside the Socialist Party the unnatural alliance which had mobilised around Mitterrand in 1971 was beginning to crack by the mid-1970s. The gap which had always separated CERES from the rest steadily widened and at the Congress of Pay in 1975 they were evicted from the leadership of the Party. This both reflected and accentuated a shift by the PS to the Right. Partly to give his rapidly expanding but fragmented party a clear sense of identity, Mitterrand began, for the first time, to emphasise the PS's continuity with the SFIO and its social democratic tradition in France — something ill-received by both the PCF and CERES.

Relations between the two supposed partners in the Union of the Left took a turn for the worse in 1975, as a result of the Portuguese crisis of that year. Marchais, the PCF leader, refused to condemn the Portuguese Communist Party which masterminded the seizure of the Socialist journal *Republica,* an act which revived doubts about the sincerity of its commitment to democracy and to co-operation with the Socialists.

The climate on the Left, nevertheless, brightened soon after. Municipal elections were due to be held in the Spring of 1977. Those elections presented a challenge to the Union of the Left and not only because it gave it an opportunity to display its strength against the Right. The SFIO had, traditionally, been firmly implanted in local government, but its hold on many municipalities was secured by alliances with the Centre. The Communists, understandably, demanded the disbanding of these alliances and the application of the Union of the Left to the local level. The issue provoked considerable dissension within the Socialist Party, with those who had always been rather lukewarm towards the policy of Left union insisting upon the right of local government representatives to make alliances with the Centre if they so pleased. A considerable body of opinion within the Party, not confined to the Left, contested this view. The union of the Left would lack credibility, they claimed, if it were not extended to the local level. This view prevailed and, with some exceptions (most notable in Gaston Defferre's fiefdom of Marseilles) the Socialists and Communists allied at the municipal elections. The Left gained sweeping victories, many Right-wing strongholds toppling before the offensive, thus the auguries for the legislative elections in 1978 seemed excellent.

But in 1977 negotiations over the updating of the Common Programme opened. To the surprise and the consternation of many, the negotiations broke down and the Communist leadership launched a campaign of vilification against the Socialist Party. (These events, and the not unsurprising defeat of the Left in the elections of 1978, are recounted at length in chapter two.) The collapse of the union of the Left — the centrepiece of Socialist strategy since 1971 — inevitably provoked disarray within the PS. The various currents within the Party draw different lessons. *CERES* and *Mitterrandistes* reaffirmed their commitment to Left union (even if it then appeared to be an elusive goal) as the only feasible strategy for the Socialist Party. Others in the PS leadership — Rocard, Mauroy and their supporters — hinted at the need for a more 'independent' line by the Party.

These differences within the Socialist leadership (i.e. between Mitterrand and his supporters and Rocard, Mauroy and their followers) over strategy became entangled with others. As a result the leadership split. At the 1979 Metz Congress, the two groups won an approximately equal number of mandates — giving the balance of power to a weakened, but now well-placed CERES. CERES threw in its lot with Mitterrand and thus, after a gap of five years, its leaders were re-admitted on to the all-important Secretariat of the Party.

The Metz Congress was bitter and divisive but the quarrel within the Party did not stop with Mitterrand's victory in the Socialist Party apparatus. Rocard and his supporters knew that they could not take control of the Party so they began to work on Rocard's undoubted popularity in public opinion to create a wave of support for his candidature which could not be resisted. After the Metz Congress the Socialist debate moved out to a wider public which created an even greater impression of division and an even greater bitterness in the Party. However, Rocard underlined that he would not oppose Mitterrand's nomination in the Party and the tidal wave of support which Rocard counted on materialised but was by no means strong enough to sweep Mitterrand aside.

For its part the Communist Party seems to have assumed that Mitterrand would run as Socialist presidential candidate and set about mounting its own presidential campaign. A good start for the Communists was made with the European elections of 1979 when they ran an anti-EEC enlargement campaign of Barnum and Bailey patriotism which got them a good vote of 20.5 per cent (to the Socialist Party's 23.5 per cent). It became fairly evident that the PCF's Secretary General, Georges Marchais, would stand in 1981 and the Communist machine was mobilised from a very early date to project the Party's candidate. As Marchais criss-crossed the country in an energetic campaign Socialist activists began to worry because they had no candidate and because the anti-Socialist tone of the Communist Party became increasingly strident. Ostensibly Marchais' campaign was an 'anti-Giscard' campaign but in fact the target was the Socialist Party, a tactic which was only modified (and then but slightly) in February 1981 when it had become clear that it was counter-productive.

Rocard tried to push the Socialist Party into an early decision, preferably in his favour but Mitterrand was not to be hurried. The Socialist Party busied itself with the enthusiastic preparation of a new programme *Le Projet Socialiste* under the close direction of J.P. Chevènement. This document had an ambiguous status in the Party and, although it was to be the base for any presidential campaign, the lack of precision about its proposals (and especially their dates) made it acceptable to all sections of the Party. In the event, therefore, the *Projet Socialiste* was a useful uniting programme, but has since been quietly forgotten.

Mitterrand and his supporters prepared the way for an election campaign which was to be short and intense and to make use of their candidate's previous experience of two major campaigns in 1965 and 1974. However before the campaign proper Rocard was not quite finished and in October 1980 he made a speech of startling ineptitude from the City Hall where he was mayor announcing that he was a 'candidate for the candidature'. This forced Mitterrand to finally declare that he would present himself for the Party's nomination and, given the grip Mitterrand has on the Party, this ended Rocard's chances of being nominated.

Once Mitterrand's position was clear Pierre Mauroy and his supporters moved behind the Party's First Secretary and Rocard was isolated (even so he seems to have hesitated about standing down). Thus from autumn 1980 Mitterrand was on course, had complete control over the Party and had no rivals within the PS. This position was confirmed when Mitterrand was nominated (there was only one nomination) as Party presidential candidate at Créteil in January 1981. There is some indication that the very pro-Rocard federations in the Party were less enthusiastic about nominating Mitterrand than were other areas but the endorsement was nonetheless overwhelming. Mitterrand had the nominating convention vote him a platform known as the '110 propositions' which became the presidential then governmental programme, though it went unnoticed at the time.

Communists had nominated Marchais, 'unanimously' as is their way, as the PCF's presidential candidate in October 1980. The Communists were thus the first of the big parties to field a candidate. However, things did not go well for the PCF campaign. To start with the Party ran a quasi-racist campaign in the winter of 1980-81 in what appears to have been an attempt to mobilise a populist electorate around the PCF's anti-immigrant banner. There were several incidents in this series but the most notorious were probably the attack on an immigrant-occupied building in Vitry with pick-axe handles and a bulldozer and the PCF demonstration outside the flat of an immigrant family alleged to have been drug trafficking (the allegation was an anonymous letter). Communist conduct over this issue was hugely condemned and Communist activists, on whom the Party is tremendously dependent especially at election times, ceased to help the Marchais campaign in their usual numbers.

Attacks on the Socialist candidate also went alongside an increasingly pro-Soviet foreign policy stance. This had been seen on a number of occasions (including the live TV broadcast by Marchais from Moscow in which he defended the invasion of Afghanistan) and it was evident in the PCF's refusal to make its view on Poland clear and its support of the USSR's SS20 missiles. If this recalled the Party's creaking Stalinism of the 1950s then this is exactly how the electorate appears to have regarded it. Moreover Georges Marchais was not a popular personality: he was difficult, aggressive, clownish and every inch a Party bureaucrat, and his past was not as squeaky clean as he claimed.

This, therefore, was the state of the Left at the beginning of the 1981 election campaign as the personalities of the Right — outgoing president Giscard d'Estaing and the Gaullist Jacques Chirac — declared their candidature. Socialists had gone through a difficult two years but were now united behind their candidate François Mitterrand and the Party, now under the First Secretaryship of Mitterrand's nominee Lionel Jospin, was a first-rate electoral organisation which was the equal of the other parties. The Communist Party was conducting an energetic campaign but was having obvious difficulties trying to persuade its own electorate to remain faithful to it despite the attractive Socialist campaign.

In fact the Socialists hardly made a mistake in their own campaign based on the slogan of 'the tranquil force' (which was Mitterrand) and which maintained an attitude of 'no concessions' to the increasingly desperate Communist demands for policy changes. There were also minor Left candidates such as the PSU's Huguette Bouchardeau, the Left Radical's Michel Crépeau and the Ecologist leader Brice Lalonde. These minor candidates probably cut into Mitterrand's vote (Socialists were particularly annoyed about Crépeau) and prevented the important psychological effect of a Mitterrand lead on the first ballot. Nevertheless as parties they served to mobilise the Left's electorate.

In the election campaign the Right presented the spectacle of a divided group whilst Giscard made a few blunders of his own. It is probable that Giscard's easy assumption of victory and the scandals of the seven year term did nothing to help him but in contrast Mitterrand took on an increasingly presidential stature. Socialists emphasised the unemployment problem in France and the need for reform in such issues as the regions, industry, human rights, and so on. Desperation was evident in Giscard's camp (especially after the first ballot) but the Socialist Party seems to have been in remarkably smooth and untroubled action throughout.

THE PRESIDENTIAL AND LEGISLATIVE ELECTIONS

Mitterrand's first ballot vote was a creditable 25.8 per cent which, if totalled with the rest of the Left, put him in a better position than the equivalent time in 1974 when Giscard had won only narrowly. Socialists had to overcome two obstacles inbetween ballots: these were a TV face-to-face with Giscard before the second round (in which Mitterrand held his own) and there was the problem of the attitude of the Communist Party.*

For the Communist Party the 1981 elections were a series of surprise packages each more startlingly horrible than the last. The first round of the presidential elections gave them a poor 15.3 per cent of the vote (their worst result since the Popular Front) and the subsequent legislative elections gave them only 44 Deputies, half of their 1978 number. Despite prior dark hints to the contrary the PCF did not call on its voters to abstain in the second ballot Mitterrand-Giscard run-off but called for a vote for the Socialist and then went into hibernation for the rest of the presidential election. This frank call for a Socialist vote was probably conditioned by the view that any other action risked a massive disavowal by its own electorate and the subsequent accusation that it had caused the Left's defeat. The PCF then took up the attitude it has maintained since: that there must be Communist participation in any Left government and that the Communists were part of the Left (this does not preclude subsequent changes of line again).

Mitterrand went on to win the run-off against Giscard with 51.75 per cent of votes cast and on his inauguration used the president's power under article 12 of the Constitution to dissolve the Assembly. This was necessary because the Assembly, which was elected in 1978, had a Right-wing majority and would not have been receptive to the new government's programme. Faced with a demoralised Right and an exhausted PCF the Socialists swept into the Assembly on a huge 37.5 per cent vote (in 1975 they had polled 22.6 per cent) and obtained an overall majority with 269 Deputies

*The TV debate between Mitterrand and Giscard was in the event not unfavourable to the Socialist (in 1974 it had been a Giscard rout) and contributed to the 'presidential', 'tranquil' image. This left the problem of the PCF.

(excluding 14 MRG). The Communist vote revived slightly to 16 per cent at the first ballot but many of their 'safe seats' fell to Socialists and their Assembly representation was reduced to half and now stands at 44.

However the Communists did have the benefit of four Ministries in the second Mauroy government formed in June after the legislative elections. These Cabinet posts (and the government's action) will be commented on below but they went to the Communists with a minimum of fuss — the 'quiet revolution' was noted by a few overseas states (like the USA who sent Vice-President Bush) but there were no scenes from France's allies.

The French Left therefore stood at the beginning of a five-year Assembly term which could be extended if the electorate returns a legislative majority after that. But the Socialists are pledged to a radical and extensive programme (see below) and the tensions on the Left of the 1970s have not disappeared so that the future is going to be troubled if nothing else. As Mitterrand then said "we have now come out of port but we are not yet in the high seas".

Footnote
1. D. Hanley, et al. *Contemporary France: Politics and Society Since 1945,* Routledge & Kegan Paul, London 1979.

CHAPTER TWO

French Socialism in the 1980s

by Eric Shaw

ELECTORATE AND MEMBERSHIP

Since 1945 — the peak of its electoral success — the old SFIO had experienced sustained and, apparently, irreversible decline. In the elections of that year, the Party had won 4½ million votes, 23.4 per cent of the poll. By 1962, its share of the vote had dwindled to 12.6 per cent (2.3 million) and then, throughout the rest of the decade, remained stagnant at around that level. Confined to its traditional bastions, failing to make a mark in the economically advancing areas in the country, the SFIO seemed to be following that once great party of the Left, the Radicals, on a slow march to oblivion.

In the 1950s, a pattern had emerged which understandably caused much concern. The pattern consisted of three trends. Firstly, the Party was becoming less and less a working class one. In fact, by the 1960s the SFIO retained its grip on only two industrial areas — the far North and Marseilles. For a party which prided itself on its proletarian origins and character, this occasioned much heart-searching. Secondly, its strength was becoming regionalised. It was disappearing as a significant political force in large stretches of the country. Thirdly, its support was concentrated in economically declining areas — either industrial (parts of the North) or rural (much of the South-West and centre). It was particularly weak, in contrast, in the biggest and most swiftly expanding industrial conurbation, the Paris region, where, together with the Radicals, it gained a meagre 12 per cent of the vote in 1967 (a good year for the Left). In other words, by the late 1960s not only was the SFIO faring badly — all the signs portended an even grimmer future.

After the elections of 1981, this picture had altered beyond recognition. All the above mentioned trends had been reversed. Table 1 sets down the changing electoral fortunes of the Socialists in the Fifth Republic (figures for the Communist Party are included for purposes of comparison).

Table 1. Socialist and Communist Vote, Parliamentary Elections in the Fifth Republic

1958	SFIO	15.5%	PCF	18.9%
1962	SFIO	12.5%	PCF	21.8%
1967	FGDS[1]	19.0%	PCF	22.5%
1968	FCDS[1]	16.5%	PCF	20.0%
1973	PS/MRG[2]	20.7%	PCF	21.3%
1978	PS/MRG[2]	24.7%	PCF	20.6%
1981	PS/MRG[2]	37.8%	PCF	16.2%

[1]FGDS = Electoral alliance comprising SFIO and Radicals.
[2]PS/MRG = Combined Vote of Socialist Party and Left Radicals (MRG).

The right-wing Radicals (included in the FGDS total) arranged alliances with the right in the 1970s. They probably accounted for 3 per cent of the FGDS vote. The MRG vote is roughly 2 per cent.

Sources: 1. *Le Matin Dossier,* Legislative Elections 1978. p.9.
2. *Revue Politique el Parlementaire,* July/August 1981.

Recovery really began after the formation of the PS in 1970. Thus a substantial increase in the Socialist vote was apparent in the 1973 elections. (A further boost was Mitterrand's success in winning over 49% of the vote in the 1974 Presidential elections). Although the Socialists performed less well than expected in 1978 (there was a short-fall of 4 per cent compared to what the opinion polls were predicting) they did pick up another 4 per cent of the poll. In the legislature elections of 1981, the Socialist achievement confounded even the most optimistic expectations.

If we compare the election results of 1978 and 1981 an interesting difference emerges. In the earlier year, the Socialist Party notched up an aggregate gain of 4 per cent. But this concealed pronounced regional variations: increases in the order of almost twice the average in some regions (e.g. Alsace-Lorraine where traditionally the Party was weak), but actual losses in others (e.g. Limousin, Languedoc, where in the past the Party has polled comparatively well).
These discrepancies were not random. The PS was advancing most rapidly in areas where previously it was weakest. There were a variety of reasons for this.

Firstly, as is discussed in more detail below, Catholics were gradually losing their reticence about voting Socialist. Secondly, and more significantly, religious practice is declining, and quite swiftly, in France, largely as a result of industrialisation and urbanisation, and the greater appeal of modern secular values. In consequence the Socialists made major inroads into such conservative Catholic bastions as Brittany and Alsace-Lorraine.

The Paris region is a special case. In 1936 (the Popular Front election) the Communist Party swept the working class suburbs of Greater Paris, displacing the SFIO as the largest left-wing party (prefiguring what was to happen in France as a whole after the war). By the 1960s, the SFIO was reduced to the status of a minor party in the country's largest industrial connurbation.

In the 1970s, the tide was reversed. A strong Socialist presence was re-established in the region and (unlike in the other areas where the SFIO had been weak) there were considerable transfers of votes from the Communists to their competitors on the Left.

On the other hand, in 1978, the PS vote stagnated, or fell, in old-established Left-wing areas in the centre and south (Limousin, Languedoc etc). These areas are largely agricultural, suggesting that voting patterns based on tradition and anti-clerical sentiment were fading.

In sharp contrast to this uneven advance, in 1981 the Socialist wave carried all before it. Socialist gains were particularly dramatic, once more, in areas which had in the past been unreceptive. In the Paris region — which includes the increasingly middle-class city of Paris and the proletarian industrial suburbs — strongholds of the Communist Party — the PS percentage more than doubled in the space of a decade, from 15 per cent in 1973, to 20 per cent in 1978 and 33 per cent in 1981. Much of the latter increment must have been at Communist expense.

In Brittany, the PS surged from 17 per cent of the vote in 1973, significantly below its national average, to 39 per cent in 1981, above its average.

However, unlike in 1978, the Party did well everywhere. The slight losses sustained in areas like Languedoc and Limousin were easily recouped and unheard-of levels of support were reached. Indeed, not only did the PS become easily the strongest in the country, it was the strongest in every region of mainland France: truly a remarkable achievement for a political force which, a decade and a half ago, seemed to be disappearing, as an effective factor, from large stretches of the country.

CLASS AND THE SOCIALIST VOTE

The Socialist Party has increased its support from all social classes. It enjoys above average backing from both the professional and managerial class and the working class. Indeed the very diversity of its electoral base inevitably raises doubts about its solidity.

By the 1960s, the SFIO, whilst retaining pockets of working class strength, was beginning to look more and more like a lower-middle-class party. And, indeed, this was, in Communist eyes, its destined role. According to this scenario, the PCF would remain *the* party of the working class whilst the Socialist contribution to the Union of the Left would be to gather in the white collar and petit bourgeois voters, the 'objective' (but subordinate) allies of the proletariat.

By the mid-1970s, the Socialist Party was clearly failing to limit itself to the role assigned to it by the PCF. Indeed, evidence that it was making inroads into the working class vote, by deepening the anxieties of the Communist leadership, played its part in the collapse of the Union of the Left.

In the months before the 1978 election, determination to hold on to its share of the working class vote seemed to be the top priority of Marchais and his colleagues. Their propaganda machine churned out the message that only the Communists could be relied upon to defend working class interests — certainly not the PS, accused of selling-out to the Right and the bourgeoisie.

Analysis of the 1978 election results indicated that Communist efforts had not been in vain. Their portion of the working class vote held more or less steady at 36 per cent (37 per cent in 1973). The Right secured 31 per cent, whilst the Socialist obtained 27 per cent — no advance whatsoever over its 1973 result. The 1978 poll appeared to demonstrate that the PS performed more effectively amongst routine white collar and professional middle-class groups. This doubtless provided some comfort to Communist leaders disturbed by the Socialist seizure of the trophy, 'largest party on the Left', in that year.

But even that consolation prize slipped from Communist hands in 1981. The Socialist share of the workers' vote jumped from 27 per cent to 44 per cent. The Communist share fell precipitously from 36 per cent to 24 per cent. This must have had the force of a body blow. An analysis[1] of the drop of the PCF proportion of votes from five occupational categories (plus the economically non-active) reveals that the Communist loss varied from 1 per cent (the non-active) to 4 per cent (small business and shopkeepers) — except for manual workers where desertions accounted for no less than 33 per cent of the 1978 total (i.e. a drop of 12 per cent). In other words, the majority of the one quarter of PCF supporters who shifted their allegience in 1981 must have been workers — the bedrock of the Party.

Turning to the Socialists, one finds that the proportionate growth in their electorate ranged from three points amongst the non-active (26 per cent to 29 per cent) to no less than 23 per cent amongst professional and managerial workers (the PS took 7 per cent of their votes in 1973, 15 per cent in 1978 and 38 per cent in 1981 — an increase of more than five hundred percent, representing an intriguing sociological phenomenon). The gain of 17 points amongst manual workers was about par with the overall Socialist result — but it transformed the Party into, in numerical terms, *the* party of the working class, with a level of popularity almost twice that of the Communists.

Table 2   The Manual Worker Vote, by Party Affiliation

	PCF	PS	The Right	Other*
1978	36%	27%	31%	6%
1981	24%	44%	29%	3%

ecologists, Far Left

Source: Revue Politique et Parlementaire, July-August 1981

The figures seem to suggest a large-scale transferral of working class votes from the Communists to the Socialists. It is, at present, impossible to say whether these electors still identified themselves as Communist but decided to shift to the PS because of dissatisfaction with their party's role in the breakdown of the Union of the Left, or for some other reason *or* whether they have terminated their Communist affiliation. Whichever is the explanation, their bonds to the Party have been loosened: whether they are restored will probably depend upon Socialist performance in government.

The Socialist electorate now includes large contingents from all social groups — its expansion being particularly rapid within those occupational categories which are waxing in numbers. However both the pace and scope of the socialist advance may make consolidation no easy matter.

Table 3   The Evolution of the Socialist Vote, by percentage of Occupational Groups

Occupation of Head of Household	*Parliamentary Elections*		
	1973	1978	1981
Agricultural	17%	17%	32%
Small business/trader	23%	23%	35%
Professional and Managerial	7%	15%	38%
White Collar Worker	23%	29%	45%
Manual Worker	27%	27%	44%
Inactive/Retired	20%	26%	29%

Source: Revue Politique et Parlementaire, July-August 1981

One further mark for the future: the Socialist advance was most rapid in the younger age groups (18-34), where the Communists sustained their biggest losses. Indeed the Communist vote held fairly steady in the 35 to 64 age groups, with a significant fall-back amongst the 65 plus. This would appear to indicate that the Communists suffered their largest defections amongst younger working class members — traditionally a core group of their electorate. Whilst the Socialists, in the aftermath of the election, were understandably elated, their Left-wings rivals would have had to search hard to find any crumb of comfort.

RELIGION AND THE SOCIALIST VOTE

The old antagonism between the Church and the Socialists has to a large extent abated. The PS is far less anti-clerical than the SFIO, whilst the Catholic Church in France is no longer one of the bulwarks of the established social order (in fact more younger priests vote for the PS than for any other party).

As has been shown, the Socialist electorate has swollen in traditional Catholic areas.

The 1978 election results, nevertheless, provided a salutory reminder that Catholic enthusiasm for the party remained tepid. At the last moment, many who (in the opinion polls) were ready to take the plunge and cast Socialist ballots took fright and returned to their customary allegiance.

Table 4 Religion and Voting

	PCF	Far Left	PS/MRG	Right	Others
Regularly practising Catholics	2	1	13	80	4
Occasionally-practising Catholics	11	—	20	61	3
Non-practising Catholics	24	3	30	37	2
No religion	49	6	29	10	4

Source: Le Nouvel Observateur 24 April 1978 (poll taken after 1978 election)

Table 4 shows quite clearly that practising Catholics were still in 1978 overwhelmingly Right-wing in orientation whilst, at the opposite end of the spectrum, the irreligious are firmly Left-wing with the categories inbetween occupying intermediate positions.

When the figures are controlled for class, the variation remains. Catholics among the working class were much more likely to vote for the Right than their irreligious fellows (and the non-Catholic middle class disproportionately backed the Left). In other words, ardent religious commitment remained a bar to left-wing voting.

It seemed, then, that Socialist gains in Catholic districts would only partly be accounted for by a shift in political alignments amongst church-goers. For a fuller explanation one must turn to changes in the social and economic structure in these areas. Large parts of the west of the country are undergoing rapid economic development and urbanisation, which is both altering the social composition of the population and secularising the popular attitudes. The weakening of attachments to the Church is encouraging an increased willingness to adopt more left-wing political beliefs.

(This progress is helped by the growing influence of the formerly Catholic, now Socialist trade union federation, the CFDT.)

At the time of writing, figures on the relationship in the 1981 elections between religious observance and voting behaviour were not available. However, on the basis of other data, it seems very likely that the link between Catholicism and political conservatism has been greatly weakened. Those religious-minded voters who failed to take the plunge and back the PS in 1978 appear to have done so, and in droves, in the legislative elections of 1981. It may well be, therefore, that one major clue to the Socialist victory is the removal, at long last, of the religious barrier which inhibited so many of its natural sympathisers in manual and white collar occupations from rallying beneath its banners.

THE SOCIALIST PARTY: MEMBERSHIP

During the long years of decline, from 1945 to 1970, the membership of the SFIO shrank remorselessly. In 1945, it stood at 355,000. By 1970, when the SFIO officially disbanded in favour of the PS, it had dwindled to 71,000 — itself an inflated figure.[2] Furthermore, a high proportion of members were local councillors: to the end the SFIO was strongly implanted in local government (with the help of the alliances it formed with the Centre and Centre-Right). In other words, in most parts of France, the grass roots of the Party had withered. Its surviving outposts were the old socialist bastion of the North (the SFIO's equivalent to Labour's North East England) and Marseilles, where the redoubtable Socialist mayor, Gaston Defferre, has dominated municipal politics for years. In fact, the Socialist federations in the three departments of the Nord, Pas-de-Calais (both in the north) and Bouches-du-Rhône (Marseilles) held almost half the membership in France.

In membership, as in voting strength, the 1970s were years of re-invigoration. By the middle of the decade membership had doubled. Further, it was more evenly spread throughout the country — new recruits were most numerous where the SFIO had been at its weakest. Hence Socialist activity revived in areas where the Party had previously been moribund.

The PS has, however, been less successful in attracting

working class members. Members and, even more so, activists are predominantly white collar. According to a survey undertaken in 1973, workers comprised only one-fifth of the membership.[3] The new recruits to the Party are largely drawn from professional and white collar occupations (as in the Labour Party in growth areas like London). The largely middle class profile holds for all sections of the Party — indeed the left-wing CERES group is notably professional in occupational background.

In view of the robustly anti-clerical tradition of the SFIO, it is significant that a high percentage of fresh adherents to the Party are practising Catholics. Probably about a third of the membership now falls into that category — and possibly more within CERES.

In the last few years, the rise in PS membership has come to a halt; it may even be falling slightly now. And whatever growth the Party sustained, its membership is still totally overshadowed by the half-million or so adherents that the Communist Party claims. At grass roots levels, the Socialists are still no match for their Communist competitors.

In addition, the Party suffers from a lack of firm base in the trade unions. Socialists dominate the large teachers union (FEN) and are well represented in the left-wing CFTD trade union federation. Socialists can also be found in the biggest trade union federation, the Communist dominated CGT, and the right-wing social democratic FO (closely aligned in earlier years with the SFIO, and fiercely anti-communist). However, unlike the PCF, the PS cannot rely on the full-hearted backing of a well organised trade union machine, nor upon the disciplined enthusiasm of thousands of trade union activists — a weakness it has tried to remedy by seeking closer links with the CFTD and by encouraging the formation of workplace branches.

The election of a Socialist President and parliamentary majority did not precipitate a rush of new recruits to the Party. But there is now the opportunity to build a mass membership party — a goal which so far only the Communists have achieved. Whether the opportunity is seized will be a test of the Socialists' capacity to exploit its recent triumphs to construct a durable party machine staffed by large numbers of committed members.

Footnotes
1. V. Wright "The French General Election of March 1978" *West European Politics,* Vol.1 (No.3), 1978, p.39.
2. See Byron Criddle, "The French Parti Socialiste" in W. Paterson and A. Thomas (eds) *Social Democratic Parties in Western Europe,* Croom Helm, 1976, p.60.
3. P. Hardouin "Sociological Characteristics of the Socialist Party, *Revue Francaisede Science Politique,* 1978, p.227.

CHAPTER THREE

Characters, Currents and Candidates

by David S. Bell

It is misleading to describe the factions or currents of opinion inside the Socialist Party in terms of the British experience; furthermore, rapid re-alignments on different issues make any description necessarily limited. Nevertheless there are identifiable nucleii around which groups in the French Socialist Party tend to congregate and some attempt to explain them will be made here as well as to place them in perspective. However it should be kept in mind that the perpetual minuet of factions of French Socialism has by no means ceased, and it can be confidently predicted that there will continue to be the occasion for numerous surprising alliances as issues are debated during Mitterrand's presidency (though they may not take the pattern of the last ten years).[1]

Before describing the main factions in the Party a point can be made about the presidential elections. Within the Socialist Party the need for a candidate who can win the presidential elections is felt at all levels. A candidate who can go beyond the immediate audience of the Socialist Party itself, and who can increase the number of winnable seats is required. There has therefore been a tendency for the groups within the Party to congregate around the pole of attraction of a presidential candidate who in the past has been François Mitterrand but from 1978 to 1980 there was a tendency to a bi-polarisation around Mitterrand and Michel Rocard.

Yet the polarisation is a tendency and no more for within the Socialist Party there are groups which take their stand on various issues and the cross-cutting effect of policy debates cannot be discounted. The element of personal power within the Party is an ever-present factor but issues do matter and Socialists do take them seriously despite what the press tends to say about the squalid nature of naked Socialist power struggles. If the element of ideology and issues is neglected the full picture of the Socialist Party will not be properly visible for various groups take their stands on issues and these can and do cut across the currents within the Party.[2]

That said, the Party has been beset by cleavages of personality and opinion since its inception. There has been ill-informed talk of Party disintegration because of factionalism but this was exaggerated because — as the table shows — there are basic agreements; the road to unity has been too long to be risked by minor disagreements within the structure of the united non-Communist Left.

(i) Mitterrand's supporters

As might be expected the biggest group within the Party are those who support its First Secretary François Mitterrand. At the 1979 Party Congress at Metz this group represented about 41 per cent of the votes of delegates and their representation on the Socialist governing body was increased to 51 per cent at Valence in 1981. Mitterrand's position is not impregnable but the chance of any coalition coming together to oppose the mild-mannered Lionel Jospin (who is Mitterrand's First Secretary) are negligible. Nevertheless precautions were taken at Metz by bringing the smaller CERES and Defferre groups (see below) into coalition to administer the Party and the Mitterrand supporters may fear troubles ahead despite the unity at the 1981 Valence Congress.

Mitterrand himself is not a life-long Socialist although he is above all the incarnation of the search for Left unity under the Fifth Republic — this explains his pre-eminent status in the Socialist Party.[3]

What Mitterrand actually believes in is more difficult to say. His Fourth Republic career, as has been noted, did not pivot on the adherence to any particularly identifiable principles. Furthermore his attempt to unite the Left is not, in his case, as it is for some, a particularly radical strategy but based on the prudential calculation that if you want to defeat the Right then you have to unite the Left. Mitterrand's writings although voluminous to a degree do not provide that much guidance because, although celebrated as a stylist, the Socialist leader does not say much in the way of concrete policy proposal. Not surprisingly, therefore, Mitterrand has been written of as a 'Florentine', a sort of Fifth Republic

Machiavelli who was not committed to a socialist vision but to a united Party in alliance with the Communists dedicated to gaining governmental power. In support of this view it can be noted that Mitterrand's personal presidential campaigns of 1974 and 1981 were very restrained, including few references to the Common Programme of the Left, and Mitterrand lisped the language of the political centre. Although his policy position is essentially pragmatic it is calculated to gain him support but leave his hands as free as possible.[4]

Mitterrand is, therefore, not a 'historic' socialist or a socialist theorist although he is a spellbinding if old-fashioned orator. Despite his distaste for the mechanics of the Party and wrangles among Socialists, his supreme achievement is the creation of the modern Socialist Party which is young, dynamic, and based on the union of the Left. Personally Mitterrand is a cold figure who, even in Socialist circles, is not called by the familiar *tu* and is friendly only with a very small number of people (this is equivalent to a Labour leader being on first name terms with nobody in the Party). In style of leadership Mitterrand is autocratic and maintains an almost complete freedom of manoeuvre — as he once said "my strategy is to remain master of my tactics". He delegates power, but never to one person (like Franklin Roosevelt) because he prefers to keep up competition amongst his advisors the better to maintain his own freedom of choice. His close political advisors, in other words, tend to be people who owe their position to Mitterrand and who do not have outside power bases — you do not compete with the leader.

The examination of the President's associates does not, in fact, bring the observer any nearer to a profile of a leadership politics. In 1979, at the congress of Metz, there was a sea-change.[5] Prior to Metz, Mitterrand was surrounded by people who had followed him through the wilderness of the 1960s and who belonged to a Fourth Republic generation — i.e. Claude Estier, Edith Cresson and so on. After Metz came the promotion of a whole group of people who entered the Party after Mitterrand and who are considerably younger than the departing leadership. These include the 'technocrats', Lionel Jospin, Paul Quilès, Laurent Fabius, and Pierre Joxe, who is one of the few 'old-timers' although he is considerably younger than the rest.

Few of the newer people have made a distinctive mark as yet. Fabius is radical and a formidable debator, a talent which he has shown on occasions defending Mitterrand at Metz, attacking the Barre budget in the Assembly and then as Budget Minister. Lionel Jospin is the Party 'First Secretary', but he is comparatively unknown to the public. He recently made an impression on Television in a debate on the history of French Socialism with Georges Marchais, a debate which was, however, more remembered for Marchais' ignorance than for the arrival of a new political star. Pierre Joxe the president of the Socialist group is a man whose career has been made in Mitterrand's shadow but he regards himself as Marxist, espouses a fundamentalist Marxism and is a committed opponent of the Common Market — he is also an admirer of the Communist dominated CGT of which he is a member.

Sociologically the Mitterrand supporters in the Party are a rough cross-section of the Party as a whole. At Metz Mitterrand had an absolute majority in 37 Federations and a plurality in 70 others and these areas of support are found south of the Loire in Aquitaine, Midi-Pyrenées and Languedoc — Rousillon, the Rhône/Alpe, Burgundy and Massif Central. This, geographically, includes the areas — the first three — of traditional socialist domination but the latter are where the Party has progressed through the 1970s. This probably reflects the determination of new comers to French Socialism to support the man who, above all, represents the new French Socialism.

There is little homogeneity in the Mitterrand group and (as he has been careful to ensure) there are no outstanding leaders. Had Mitterrand declined to present himself as the candidate for 1981 the group would have little coherence and none of the associates has the stature of a potential president.

Associated with the Mitterrand leadership are a number of minor groups. Most important is the Gaston Defferre group. This is the Bouches-du-Rhône Federation based on the city of Marseilles, of which Interior Minister Defferre is mayor, and where municipal Socialism of a visceral anti-Communist kind has remained important despite the Socialist collapse of the

50s.[6] Defferre is associated with de-colonisation and an anti-Communist centrism of the mid-1960s but he was instrumental in bringing Mitterrand into the Socialist Party and has supported him closely ever since. His Federation was split by the defection of his lieutenant Emile Loo to the Mauroy current at Metz (for which he was sharply downgraded by Defferre) but he still brought a vital 6 per cent to Mitterrand's group. Apart from Defferre there are a few personalities — like Arthur Notebart — with local and somewhat eccentric reputations who have thrown their weight behind Mitterrand in the Party struggle since 1978. These are minor, however.

(ii) Michel Rocard's 'social democrats'

This group is of importance in the Socialist Party because it is centred on a possible president, Michel Rocard. Now Minister of the Plan, Rocard is a figure of no little importance in French politics on the Left not just because, from about 1978 to 1980, he was consistently the most popular figure of the opposition in opinion polls but also because he represents a distinctive technocratic, 'Mendesiste' moderate Socialist Left which is still popular in the country. In fact the last mentioned characteristic explains why he is the man the Communists love to hate as the very image of 'revisionism' and why he is popular with the electorate of the Centre and even of the Right.[7]

Rocard's career has been a complicated one. A well-placed, well educated ENA graduate, he was in the old SFIO before leaving over disagreements about the policy to the Algerian war and he joined the PSU which was then a strictly reformist party. While the SFIO was declining the PSU picked up disillusioned members of the non-Communist Left and it grew in influence, if not greatly in size. In 1967 Rocard became National Secretary leader of this organisation and endeavoured to build a reformist, disciplined but imaginative Left in counterpoint to the sclerotic SFIO of the 60s. The presidential elections of 1969 provided the spring-board for Rocard's national ambition and he polled well (3.7 per cent to the Socialist Party's 5.1 per cent); later in the year he was able to defeat de Gaulle's Prime Minister Couve de Murville in the Yvelines constituency — a famous victory.

Yet, successful as Rocard was in the PSU, this faction ridden, torn and divided Party was not the vehicle that Rocard wanted. For one thing the May '68 events had led to an influx of new members who swung the centre of gravity of the PSU violently to the Left — quite out of step with Rocard's supporters. The late 1960s and early 1970s saw the development of a PSU which was well to the left of other Left wing parties — it was almost *gauchiste* in fact. Rocard kept control only because of its divisions but at the risk of speaking a somewhat double language (Left to the activists, Right to the electors) and because he was the most eminent PSU figure. Rocard inherited from the PSU his exceptionally close relations with the Left Catholics and the CFDT union Federation as well as a close-knit group of supporters throughout France.

Rocard's PSU position was becoming increasingly difficult in the early 1970s. He helped Mitterrand as an economic aide in the 1974 presidential elections and this was at odds with the general line of his own PSU. In October 1974 Pierre Mauroy engineered the entry of Rocard into the Socialist Party in the Assises. One of the last major figures of the non-Communist Left thus entered the Socialist Party leaving only the marginal groups outside though it must be said that Rocard failed to bring his own PSU with him. In particular, the CFDT unions did not make use of the occasion to enter into a formal association with the Socialists.

Rocard did not immediately play a big role in Socialist Party affairs. He seems to have concluded that it was not seemly to enter a Party only to start causing problems for the leadership and in any case Mitterrand was too strong at that time. Rocard's supporters moved in several directions. Some, whose main concern was workers' control, joined CERES, other who had specific skills moved into posts in the Socialist apparatus. Therefore Rocard, despite his reservations about the Common Programme, was active but not obstructive in the Party from 1974-1978 all the while laying the ground for a 'social democratic' wing within the Party — however Rocard does not use the term 'social democratic' himself.

In 1977 at the Socialist Congress at Nantes Rocard's speech spelt out the lines of his policy: he emphasised the role of the market and market forces and condemned the economic irrationality of the Left. Much of this went unheeded at the time but after the elections of 1978 he took the opportunity to reiterate his distinctive views with the strong implication that he could offer an alternative to the 'archaic' Left. All this was taken to be an implicit attack on Mitterrand and in general signalled a rising, or reactivation, of the Rocard support around an alternative to Mitterrand as Party candidate.

Rocard's group does seem to be a 'social democratic' movement within the Party but based on the undoubtedly popular figure of the Minister of the Plan. If Rocard's rhetoric of workers' control is stripped away, and this does mean very little, what remains is a free market, mixed economy Scandinavian-style socialism, a technocratic managerial socialism which claims that through state intervention it can restore the competitive position of the French economy whilst protecting the weaker sections of society — such as the young, the sick, the unemployed and so on — in a way which Giscard's France did not. Whether this vision is genuine or not, and CERES sees in this only a left-wing Giscardianism, it is clearly not acceptable to the Communist Party which wants to go far beyond such 'tinkerings' with capitalism.

In styles the contrast between Rocard and Mitterrand is particularly great. Whereas Mitterrand is cold, distant, and works alone, Rocard has an immediate charm, is approachable, and very much part of a team. Many have said that Rocard is so much the man of a team that he hardly exists and that he is the creation of media-minded technocrats. There is something in this. Rocard has developed a style and a presence on TV and in the press with an assiduity which is rare amongst French politicians let alone on the Left. A development from the motor-biking presidential candidate of 1969 to the well-dressed statesman figure of the 1980s is very evident and is the result of the teamwork around Rocard. Likewise his TV appearances and his use of a clear precise language is the result of hard work and his various pronouncements are 'placed' to have the desired effect in the media. These 'tailorings' of the candidate to fit the modern media have been taken to imply a similar 'doctoring' of political views by his opponents.[8]

Sociologically the Rocard group is highly interesting. It is

spread throughout the party and in 1979 there were very few
Federations where it fell below 20 per cent with the
strongholds being in the west — Brittany, Normandy, and the
Loire — areas with a strong Catholic tradition where the
CFDT is well established.[9] These are also areas where
Mitterrand was weak and which are relative newcomers to
Socialism, the areas of the Centre-Left where the Party
developed in the 1970s and where Rocard's ideas find a
strong echo. As noted, this group is often associated with the
old PSU and with the CFDT unions but Rocard also has
support amongst local government Socialists and in the
Senate where Rocard's suggestions that he could provide an
alternative after the débâcle of 1978 were quite well received.
However, Rocard's group has been reduced to 15 per cent
and has lost numerous key posts.

The Rocard current has a number of influential supporters
including Gilles Martinet (of the *Nouvel Observateur*, and
now Ambassador in Rome), J.P. Cot (a young Minister),
Patrick Viveret and so on. Rocard's contacts in the unions
and in the working class — it should be noted — are probably
more extensive than any other Socialist leader and his group
has a genuinely popular support although, like all French
Socialism, it is principally an affair of the new middle class.
The Rocard group is not as well organised as CERES but it
does have a network of contacts across the country, and its
own headquarters, its own journal *Faire,* and enthusiastic —
if not always helpful — support, from the newspaper *Le
Matin.*

Rocard repeatedly stated that he would not try to contest
the Party nomination against Mitterrand. However this was
slightly disingenuous because Rocard's strategy was to create
a popular pro-Rocard movement which would place
Mitterrand in the impossible position of running against the
'people's choice'. Although Rocard was more popular than
Mitterrand this weight of opinion was not created and as a
result Rocard's position within the Party is emphatically a
minority one and his own position is highly precarious.

Rocard's technocratic socialism *à la suedoise* has many
friends and the freshness of his approach found recruits in a
Party reeling from the collapse of the strategy of Left union
in 1978 as a consequence of Communists' intransigence. The

moderate reformism, respect for Keynesian economics, liberalism on social issues and contempt for many traditional socialist themes (ironically the plan was, according to Rocard, 'mere poetry') are all more severely revisionist than any other major figure on the French Left has been for many years, although it has been suggested here that in practice the difference from Mitterrand is minimal.[10]

(iii) Pierre Mauroy

Prime Minister Mauroy is the mayor of Lille (a long-time Socialist strong-hold) and was himself the Party's number two from the mid-1960s until Metz. First under the SFIO leader Guy Mollet and then under François Mitterrand (who he brought into the Party) he was king-maker, a role which he appears destined to continue for Rocard with whom he formed a close alliance in 1978, although they have since fallen out somewhat. Mauroy's primary concern has been with the Party's organisation, structure and strength and he is known as an administrator who has come up through the Socialist Party ranks. But being mayor of a major industrial city is no negligible office in France and Mauroy along with Mitterrand and Rocard is one of the three major figures of the French Left — according to opinion poll data.

Like CERES, the Mauroy current within the Party undoubtedly suffered from the bi-polarization of Socialists around Mitterrand and Rocard in 1979. Mauroy broke with the Mitterrand leadership in 1978 over Rocard's bid to become the 1981 Socialist candidate for the presidentials. Paradoxically Mauroy's main theme has been Party unity, and had it not been for his emotional *tour de force* on this subject at Metz, his group would probably have been sunk. As it was the Mauroy group kept some 15 per cent of activist support and includes some very distinguished figures of French Socialism (M.R. Pontillon, Alain Savary the first First Secretary of the Party, etc) and a large number of young people such as Françoise Gaspard and Jean Le Garrec. As the Prime Minister's group its importance has increased and it is now probably some 20 per cent or so inside the Party.

In terms of sociology the Mauroy group was being continually squeezed: caught in the position of constituting a minority split to lobby for unity *against* Mitterrand, the real

unifier of French Socialism, and in trying to be the honest
broker between Rocard and the leadership whilst being a
pressure group for Rocard. This is illustrated by the number
of Federations that have minority Mauroy factions and even
in Mauroy's own Nord Federation his current had only 40 per
cent in 1979. However there has been the beginning of a
Mauroy organisation with meetings and canvassing of the
regional Socialists for support. Yet the Prime Minister's
group faced a difficult enough position in his Nord
Federation in 1979 and a good deal of ground had to be made
up against the gradient of Party bi-polarization although it is
now secure.

Mauroy's group is often spoken of as the Party's Right. It
is certainly the case that their positions on workers' control,
the European Community, the Atlantic Alliance, planning
and the economy places them amongst the more reformist
groups in the Party. But a reservation should be made here
because they are more radical than many Rocard or Jacques
Delors supporters (on the plan for example). Furthermore on
some issues such as internal Party organisation they are allied
with CERES, an alliance which at times has its curious
aspects. The Nord is the area of Socialist anti-clericalism and
anti-Communism and whereas these attitudes have by no
means faded away they are no longer predominant within the
Party nationally.

(iv) CERES

CERES is usually spoken of as the Party's Left which is how
it regards itself. Workers' control, Left union with the
Communists, and a visceral form of nationalism are its
distinctive policies but these are discussed in some detail by
David Hanley in Part Two.

For the immediate, a few remarks could be made about
CERES strength which may be about 20 per cent after the
1981 Valence Congress but which was 27.3 per cent at the
Nantes Congress of 1977. Internal disputes and the squeezing
effect of the Party's bipolarisation have damaged the group
although now that it has regained its place on the Secretariat
it can be expected to progress somewhat. Many CERES
supporters are Catholic or lapsed Catholics and it is very
much a middle-class group with strong intellectual support. It

ISSUES AND GROUPS AT THE 1979 FRENCH SOCIALIST CONGRESS

Main Congress Groups

The four Main Issues	Mauroy	Rocard	Mitterrand	CERES
Left Union	call for a 'new balance of forces', want a clear engagement by PCF to support a Left government. No return to 1972-1978, want a public debate		wants common action with the PCF which will bring them round	Common programme and action with the PCF.
	All agree on the need for Left Union with the PCF and all refuse centre alliances			
Economic Policy	Pro-planning against Rocard's 'economism', but against the primacy of politics	anti-planning, pro-market and against 'politics First'	pro-planning anti-market primacy of politics	pro-planning anti-market workers' control
	All call for a 'break' with capitalism			
Europe	Pro-supranational	Pro-European	'Only the Rome Treaty — no more'	Anti-enlargement + Anti-supranational
Party Organisation	Activist freedom and minority rights	Collegiate leadership, minority rights, activist freedom	Unity, discipline and coherence	Minority expression important and activist freedom
	All want certain sectors (like factory sections) to work better and more efficiently			

is also a group which has stronger support amongst activists than it does in elected bodies regional or national.

This concludes the section on Party groups. These currents could change in the future and there are some minor groups which have not been described and could change affiliation during the coming events, but for the most part the Party is polarised around President Mitterrand and his supporters.[11]

SOCIALIST PARTY STRATEGY

French Socialism faced a seemingly straightforward problem. If it wanted to become a Party of government then it had to defeat the conservative coalition which had aligned itself behind three successive Presidents — de Gaulle, Pompidou and then Giscard d'Estaing. Conservative parties are no new thing in Britain or America but the French have not before witnessed a stable, organised, modern, Republican Right which is capable of winning elections regularly and which has in fact done so since de Gaulle came to power in 1958. This conservative coalition behind Giscard disintegrated because of its tendency to internal quarrels in 1981.

Under the Fourth Republic in the 1950s Socialists participated in governments of the centre which sometimes included conservatives or independents but it is now clear that this situation will not return. One of the first people to draw the logical consequences of this need to defeat the Right-wing coalition was Mitterrand. As against those who argued that large sections of the Centre could be enticed away from the conservative Right (those Centrists who at one time supported de Gaulle) Mitterrand asserted the need for an alliance with the Communist Party.

Communists had, of course, been excluded from the 1950s governments of the Fourth Republic and the Cold War had forced them into a position of isolation or ghettoisation — yet the Communists composed about one-fifth of the electorate and the Right could not be defeated without Communist support because on the second ballot the non-Socialist Left and Centre constituted but 38 per cent at the very best. On purely vote getting, utilitarian criteria, therefore, the Communists were an indispensable part of any Left which hoped to defeat the conservative Right. But the Communists were still greatly mistrusted by the rest of the

French electorate and any association with the Communists would put off Centrist voters whose support was also needed to defeat the Right.[12]

Here was paradox indeed: the Socialists needed the support of the Communists but Communist support chased away the floating voter whose support was needed quite as much as the Communists. Before Mitterrand the solutions to the squaring of this circle tended to concentrate on the building of a Centre Party based on the Socialists, but including Christian Democrats and anti-Gaullist liberals, to create a massive Centre-Left formation capable of dictating terms to the Communist Party from a position of great strength i.e. a big popular vote, strong organisation and genuine reformist policies. However the differences between the parties of the non-Gaullist Centre were too great and this policy ultimately foundered on severe practical differences. Centre parties then drifted hither and thither in the 1960s, some joining the Right coalition and others joining the renovated Socialist Party.

Mitterrand's view was that the Left should first make an agreement with the Communists and then move to capture the vital Centre votes from the Right by showing the Socialists to be an expanding, reforming, well-organised Party not dependent upon the whim of the Communists. The problems presented by the application of such a strategy in the 1960s were manifold and not the least of them was that Mitterrand was not, and never had been, a Socialist: the SFIO distrusted Mitterrand and was almost as difficult as other groups. However Mitterrand was supported — *faute de mieux*, it could be said — by both the SFIO and the Communists in the presidential elections of 1965 where he achieved the unthinkable by pushing de Gaulle onto a second ballot run-off where he managed an excellent 45 per cent. Thus began Mitterrand's long march to Left unity on the basis of an alliance with the Communist Party.[13]

There were a few years of comparative success before the Mitterrand experiment came to pieces after May 1968 and the invasion of Czechoslovakia.[14] But, even in the years of apparent immobility, things were happening. The SFIO decided to dissolve itself and reconstitute a new party — the *Parti Socialiste* — which was based on alliance to the Left with the Communists. In 1971 Mitterrand became First

Secretary of the then weak Socialist Party which he started to renovate internally and which he moved into signing a common programme or common manifesto with the Communists (in 1972). At this point the old criticisms were once again voiced, namely: that the Communists would take over the Socialists, that the Centre voters would never accept to vote for such an 'alliance against nature', and that the Left was doomed to impotence.

In fact in the mid-1970s the opposite happened. New life was infused into the Socialist Party which became the rallying point for the non-Communist Left and the Socialists proved to be the growing and attractive part of the alliance — at one point opinion polls were putting the Socialists at 30-33 per cent similar to the vote which they achieved in 1981. Far from frightening the anti-Gaullist but uncommitted vote the union of the Left, to the benefit of Mitterrand's Socialists, proved to be the key to success, expansion, new blood, new life and to lift French Socialism into the ranks of the major French parties.

What happened after this is now well known. Attractive as it was to the floating non-Communist but anti-Conservative voters the new Socialist dynamism proved unacceptable to the Communists who started a bitter polemic with the Socialists in late 1974 which continued until the 1981 presidential elections (with varying degrees of violence). However, for the Socialists, the dilemma still remains that they cannot dispense with Communist support but must still find some way of keeping the Communists behind them as they reach out for the uncommitted vote they also need.

Rocard tried to suggest that there was an alternative and in the debacle of post-March 1978 this found ready ears.[15] What, in effect, Rocard said was that the Socialist Party had a proven potential for growth with the middle class and Centrist voters and that the Party should have used this potential to create a larger unified Socialist Party which would be reformist — but not revolutionary — and which would probably be very attractive to those who now vote Communist. The Communist Party would be diminished in size, because it would lose voters and activists to the Socialist Party capable of bargaining from a position of great strength. But the problem here was that, even if this were to

be the outcome, would the Communists accept being dictated
to by anybody, let alone the Socialist Party under Rocard's
influence? In effect this is what happened in the 1981
elections when the Socialist Party made very good showings
and the PCF polled very badly: the Communists were then
forced to swing behind the Socialist Party and Mitterrand
under the threat of punishment from their own electorate.

SOCIALISM IN FRANCE AFTER THE 1981 ELECTION VICTORY

As soon as Mitterrand took office as President in May 1981 a
new Socialist government under Pierre Mauroy as Prime
Minister was constituted. The first government gave no
indications of particular bias in one direction or another and
seemed to be carefully balanced between different groups in
the Socialist Party. A possible exception to this is the Rocard
group: Rocard himself was made a Minister of State but in
the relative backwater of the Planning Ministry, there were
other Rocardians in the government (J.P. Cot, for example)
but they were not prominent. Other Ministries were
distributed between the various currents in the Party, with the
main part going to the Mitterrand supporters, and there were
Left Radical appointments.

The second Mauroy government was formed after the
Assembly elections: in this government a few Ministers who
were not making the desired impression were removed (thus
Joxe left Industry and Bombard the Environment) and four
Communist Ministers were brought in: C. Fiterman, A. Le
Pors, J. Ralite, M. Rigout. A political agreement of no great
substance was concluded between the PCF and the Socialist
Party to make this possible but the entry of the Communists
made no strong impact on public opinion — the PCF had,
after all, just lost an election and were in a very weak
position. Other notable appointments in the French Socialist
government include Jacques Delors as Economics Minister
and Laurent Fabius as delegate Budget Minister. The Finance
Ministry forms a centre of power which has not quite been
co-ordinated with other government action and these two
Economics Ministers are reputed to be at cross-purposes. The
Foreign Minister was ex-EEC Commissioner Claude
Cheysson; the former head of the Renault nationalised car

company, P. Dreyfus moved to the Industry Ministry after Joxe; the CERES leader J.P. Chevènement was made Minister of State for Research; Mme Questiaux took charge of National Solidarity (until replaced by Pierre Bérégoroy in June 1982) and Mme Cresson became Minister of Agriculture. Michel Jobert the independent Gaullist was made Foreign Trade Minister and Michel Crepeau the Left Radical was made Environment Minister in the two main non-Socialist appointments.

Within the Socialist Party the movement of the major figures to government meant considerable changes as did the election of a large number of new Deputies. However, the disputes which had racked the Socialist Party in the past became secondary after Mitterrand's victory on the second round of the presidential elections. The challenge from Rocard which was centred on the presidential nomination faded but did not disappear because Rocard, and the Rocardians, had policy disagreements which were liable to surface later and they did in fact do so when Rocard made critical comments about budget over-spending in the autumn of 1981.

There was a feeling of Party unity after the elections which meant that the Congress which, by statutes, had to be held in 1981 would be a Party unity Congress. No separate motions were presented from the different currents of the Party only a single unitary text was tabled with a few amendments from individuals. This was an unprecedented position and not one which was foreseen in the Party constitution because the various motions are used to elect the leadership for the next two years.

In these conditions the leadership of the various organs, Federations, and national structures were nominated by the outgoing after extenside bargaining. In this process the Rocard group were the principal losers and Mitterrand's supporters gained an absolute majority. Mitterrand's supporters tried to get the Rocard group to present a motion to the Congress to gauge their support but the Rocard group, probably correctly, decided that times were not propitious for such a move. Therefore the 1981 Congress at Valence was characterised by unity from the start.

It may well be that the future disputes in the Socialist Party will take place along the same lines of cleavage as in the past: one obvious possibility is the Social Democrat or moderate reticence about the current 'pace' of Pierre Mauroy's government which was expressed by Economics Minister Jacques Delors in December 1981 and which split Rocard from the Prime Minister in the same month on the issue of budget spending. This is an eventuality which was foreseen by the Mitterrand supporters and this is one of the reasons for clamping down on the Party organisation.

Yet the Party faces other unresolved problems which do not fall into this model. The parliamentary Party has exerted its muscles *vis-à-vis* the government over a number of issues (immigrant laws and local radio, for example) and the government has had to negotiate. Government difficulties over the new immigrant laws were caused by a group of Deputies which included M. Bernard Derosier (a head of the Mauroy current in the Party) and are therefore not a simple extension of the old factional disputes. These problems will be worked out by negotiation in the future and they are not debilitating for the Party although they are new forms of dispute.

Similarly the Party itself is undecided as to whether it is a supporting organisation for the government (disparagingly called *godillots)* or whether it should have some other role. The Party had not decided at Valence whether it was the tribune for the new Socialist government or the tribune for public opinion. This was shown in the difference of tone in the Valence Congress between, on the one hand Quilès who talked of Robspierre and revolution, and the government view, put by J.P. Chevènement, which is one of State authority and calm realism. The Party Congress was one which pushed the government in a more radical direction despite the reticence of the government Ministers who talked of national solidarity against the activists' pressure.

Lionel Jospin, the Party First Secretary, who is very close to Mitterrand will face problems over the next two years as he tries to bring the Party into the political arena as Mitterrand's supporting group. Jospin is now installed as First Secretary but the Party's problems as a government Party are only just beginning.

Footnotes

1. See Criddle, *op.cit.*
2. J.F. Bizot *et alia, Au Parti des Socialistes,* Paris, 1975.
3. V. Wright and H. Machin "The French Socialist Party: Success and the Problems of Success" *The Political Quarterly,* Vol. 46, Jan-March, 1975, pp.36-52.
4. See F.L. Wilson *The French Democratic Left,* 1963-1969, Stanford, 1974.
5. *Le Monde,* 6 April 1979.
6. J.F. Bizot *loc. cit.*
7. Rocard's view of 'social democracy' can be found in *Le Matin,* 7 June 1979 "La social — démocratie et nous". See below.
8. See *L'Effet Rocard,* Paris, 1980.
9. See *Regards sur . . . Le Parti Socialiste,* 1977, No.3, "Les catholiques n'ont plus peur", pp.69-71.
10. J.F. Bizot *loc.cit.*
11. M. Charzat *et alia Le CERES — un combat pour le socialisme,* Paris, 1975.
12. *Le Monde,* 14 April 1978 and the CP view in *L'Humanité* 5 April and 20 March 1978.
13. F.L. Wilson "The Left in French Politics" in *Contemporary French Civilisation,* (Bozeman, M.T.) winter 1978, pp.205-29.
14. H.G. Simmons *French Socialists in search of a role, 1956-1967,* London, 1970.
15. C.F. Rocard's interview in *Le Matin,* 12 March 1979.

CHAPTER FOUR

The Structure and Organisation of the Socialist Party

by David S. Bell

PARTY ORGANISATION

The French Socialist Party organisation is complicated and to those familiar with Labour Party organisation it will not present many points of comparison. However because Party organisation (and internal Party democracy) is under considerable discussion in the Labour Party and because it is important in the French Socialist Party — it is still a contested issue in France — it is useful to review the subject in some detail.[1]

As a preliminary a number of points could be made. First the French Socialist Party lacks any formal links with the union federations. The *Force Ouvrière* (a union federation that split away from the Communist-run CGT in the late 1940s) is not big or well organised but it has historically been close to the Socialists, and its leaders are usually Socialists.[2] But with the union of the Left and the association with the Communists of the 1970s the Socialists and *Force Ouvrière* drifted apart. In the 1970s the Leftist CFDT union federation grew considerably to its present 500,000 membership and although it was hoped by many Socialists that some link might be established this has never materialised although Socialists are well represented in the union — it has been close to the Socialists in the 1970s. FEN, the teachers' union, is the most Socialist union and always has been, although it is not quite so large as other federations; Socialists are traditionally strongly represented amongst schoolteachers and the Fifth Republic is no exception. Moreover the Socialists do have members and are represented in the biggest union federation, the CGT, though Communist Party views swamp all others in that organisation.

Secondly, the structure of the Socialist Party — despite what is often said — demands a higher degree of participation and activity than is assumed in the UK.[3] French politics is a very intense and absorbing affair and ordinary members are called upon to vote, discuss, attend conferences/meetings, and decide more than are British Party members. The consequences of this are not always straight-forward. Activists do become disillusioned and do not have the time, or the inclination, to read through the truly enormous flow of literature which the Party and its various factions continue to pour out. In other words although inner-Party discussions take place on certain points and are often highly abstruse the activists are not necessarily aware of all the issues and all the disputes. Perversely therefore, the effect of the intellectualisation of all the issues and of the interminable discussions is to further personalise and oversimplify choices.

Thirdly the Party is verbose to an incredible degree. Not only the Party but each group within the Party has its private press. Thus there are bulletins, journals, digests, policy statements etc, etc, from practically every quarter (although some are better produced than others). In the national media there is the daily *Le Matin* and weekly *Nouvel Observateur* which are pro-Socialist (and pro-Rocard) and in the provinces papers like *Le Provençal* owned by Marseilles' Socialist mayor Gaston Defferre. Apart from these there are the Rocardian journal *Faire,* the CERES *Non!,* the bulletin *Pour L'Union* of Pierre Joxe, the Poperen *Synthèse — Flash* all from the factions as well as the Party's own *Le Poing et La Rose, L'Unité* (like *Labour Weekly)* and specialist publications for different sections of the Party — agriculture, regions etc. There has been *Combat Socialiste* a 1981 election Party daily although this was one of the causes of the split between Pierre Mauroy and François Mitterrand and has now disappeared for lack of support.

Fourthly, as the above may indicate, factionalism (although not called such) is an endemic problem in French Socialism and factions are paradoxically both better organised and more mercurial than equivalents in the Labour Party. Attempts have been made to curb this factionalism, notably by disciplining factional set-ups if they become too well organised such as to constitute a 'party within a party'. This happened to CERES (see the chapter below, by David

Hanley) after the Nantes Congress of 1977 but Rocard has also been accused of building a similar apparatus. Occasionally there are problems of discipline and from time to time there are expulsions but although these are more frequent than in the Labour Party there is no question of 'white anting' or infiltration as people have suggested there is in Britain.

Fifthly this is a middle class and intellectual Socialist Party very much dominated by University, College and School-teachers and many people from management (particularly the prestigeous colleges the French equivalent of Oxbridge). Although it has been suggested that these people are the sons and daughters of workers it nevertheless remains the case that the input from those of modest origins is minimal. This brings up a subsidiary point that the Socialists in almost all matters, and organisations is no exception, are looking over their shoulders at the Communists. For the French Socialists, therefore, on matters of organisation, efficiency, activity, size, the comparison is not with the Right or with overseas Socialists but with the Communist Party.

It should also be noted that since the 1971 Epinay Congress François Mitterrand has been the unchallenged leader and until the 1978-1980 period his style of leadership, which had something in common with Mollet's party bossism-style of management, was becoming increasingly autocratic. Yet the almost sovereign power which Mitterrand held was based on consent: Mitterrand was (until recently) the only candidate of presidential stature, he almost won the 1974 elections, he brought the Party from the depths, to supreme power and gave French Socialism hope for the future. However Mitterrand was an outsider, never in the SFIO, he joined the PS only in 1971, and relied on the big Federations of Pas-de-Calais and the Bouches-du-Rhône to provide the solid basis for his leadership until Metz in 1979. It is not, of course, true that Mitterrand is insecure in his command, quite the contrary, nevertheless the current of opinion which made him the supreme figure lost some force after the 1978 elections and therefore Party activists and factions were not quite so inclined to go without 'their' say as they have been since the victory of 1981. Hence there are now distinct differences of opinion on organisation (see below).

PARTY STRUCTURE

In the French Socialist Party organisation follows closely on SFIO and is set out in the July 1969 statutes decided at the Issy congress: Article 4 describes the basic 'building block', the *section* (minimum size — 5), which is based on the lowest local government unit, the commune or, in big towns, the *arrondissement* (roughly equivalent to the ward) but there are provisions for workplace sections as well (see below). These units elect their officers, control their finances and send delegates to Party conferences. A very big percentage of their time is spent raising money but they also debate motions on policy and resolutions as they arise.[4]

Above the section are the 96 Departmental (approximately the 'county') Federations (Article 10) which must contain at least fifty (Article 12) members and five sections; this level is a most important unit of the *Parti Socialiste* for two reasons, one practical, one organisational. Practically French Socialism has been dominated by the big Federations of Pas-de-Calais, Bouches-du-Rhône (Marseilles-Aix), and Nord (Lille urban district), since the war. The French Socialist Party after 1956 almost ceased to exist in the rest of the country (including Paris) and the intense Socialist activity took place in these restricted areas. This fact is reflected in their current disproportionate size of around 12,000 members each. They are also the main working class Federations.

Organisationally, the Federations decide local party policy and send delegates to National meetings, they also mandate delegates to these — receiving votes in proportion to paid-up members.

A Federation receives (Article 30) one delegate for every 250 members but smaller Federations do get a weighted vote: 50-100 = one, 100-250 = two. Federations are the place where policy is thrashed out prior to national decisions, they are the expression — very often — of distinct and old traditions in French Socialism. The Bouches-du-Rhône is Gaston Defferre's Federation, Paris was 'controlled' by CERES, and the Nord has a distinctive approach to socialist problems in France stretching back to the 19th century (to Jules Guesde and the municipal Socialists of the 1900s).

Proportional representation is, in contrast to the old SFIO, applied throughout the French Socialist Party organisation.

FRENCH SOCIALIST PARTY: ORGANISATION[4]

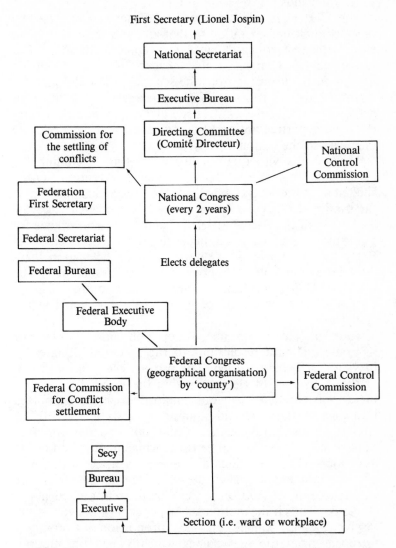

First Secretary (Lionel Jospin)

National Secretariat

Executive Bureau

Directing Committee (Comité Directeur)

Commission for the settling of conflicts

National Control Commission

National Congress (every 2 years)

Federation First Secretary

Federal Secretariat

Federal Bureau

Federal Executive Body

Elects delegates

Federal Congress (geographical organisation) by 'county'

Federal Commission for Conflict settlement

Federal Control Commission

Secy

Bureau

Executive

Section (i.e. ward or workplace)

Federations are no exception to this rule. Reflecting the national structure there are three levels in the Federation: the Federal Secretariat, the Federal Bureau and the Federal Executive; they all depend on the Federal Congress and there is, on top, a Federation 'First Secretary'. The First Secretary

of the Federation is nominated by the Federal Bureau which
in turn depends on the Federal Executive.

This latter is elected by the Federal Congress by
proportional representation so that all the shades of opinion
within the departmental party are represented on it. The
Departmental Congress meets every two years and is
composed of delegates from the sections, these delegates in
turn reflect grass roots opinion and disagreements amongst
activists where these exist. Federal Congresses, therefore,
elect the departmental party organisation and they delegate
members to the national party meetings.

There are a variety of national meetings including the
National Congress and the National Convention. Often
spoken of as the sovereign body of the French Socialist Party,
the National Congress meets every two years to elect the
leadership of the Party (Article 28) and is extremely powerful
as the ultimate decision-making body. Each Federation of the
Party has a vote at the Congress and its delegation there
disposes of one vote (see above) for every 25 members. The
National Congress elects a Directing Committee (CD —
Comité Directeur) on the basis of resolutions voted at the
Congress.

Thus different currents of opinion may jointly, or
separately, submit resolutions to the National Congress if
they cannot be composited. The process gives an indication
of the main lines of cleavage within the Party: before 1981
there was a heterogeneous majority which supported
François Mitterrand, and a minority (around a fifth of
Congress mandates) which, while not exactly opposing
Mitterrand, emphasised some issues which made a composite
impossible. These motions also annexe a list of signatories
and a number of these are voted onto the Directing
Committee, in proportion to the vote the motion gets at the
Congress. Thus if the motion get 16 per cent of the vote it will
be given an approximate equivalent proportion of Committee
members from the first names which signed the motion.
Proportional election by resolution in this manner was
insisted upon by CERES and was one of the innovations of
the 1971 National Congress at Epinay when Mitterrand's
'coup' took place but it runs counter to the post-war
Molletiste tradition because it supposedly encourages

factionalism.

National Congresses are prepared in a complicated manner. First the resolutions are submitted to Federal Congresses, then to the whole Party, and then (Article 33) two months before the National Congress an 'information conference' is held at which all the motions are presented by advocates. This done the Directing Committee tries to composite the various motions which are then sent back to the Federal Congresses. They are discussed, voted upon, and then the Federal Congress mandates its delegates to the National Congress. Between National Congresses, extraordinary Congresses can be held to deal with particular matters where there is disagreement in the Directing Committee (for example the Bondy "Europe" Congress), or on issues which the Congress thinks the Party should discuss.

Between National Congresses the Directing Committee meets every month (Article 43) to apply Congress policy, direct the Party and generally oversee matters. Article 47 of the Party statutes ensures that the Directing Committee keep close to opinion by making provision for a National Convention, composed of a delegate from each Federation, to meet every two years and this is expected to keep the Congress decisions respected. In the past the clash has not been between Directing Committee and Congress but between Directorate and parliamentarians (see below), a conflict that the old SFIO brusquely resolved when, in 1956, Guy Mollet as General Secretary became Prime Minister and the Party was subordinated to the government.

There are 131 members of the Directing Committee. However this Committee elects a smaller Executive Bureau (Article 41) of 27 which is the main administrative organ of the Party. Within the Executive Bureau are the Secretariat.

In general there are 15 or so National Secretaries who conduct policy in specific areas and they have Assistant Secretaries who also look after policy areas. In 1981 after the Valence Congress the new secretariat was as follows:

First Secretary: Lionel Jospin (Deputy);
Elections: Jean Poperen (Party number two);
Organisations and Federations: Paul Quilès (Deputy for
  Paris XIII);

Political Education: Gérard Delfau;
External Relations: Marcel Debarge;
Communication and Publicity: Jean-Claude Routier;
Research: Jean Pronteau;
Public Sector: Michael Charzat (CERES);
Information and Party Membership: Christine Mora;
Environment and Quality of Life: Michel Pezet;
Culture: Didier Motchane (CERES);
Local Politics: Pierre Guidoni (CERES);
Liberties and Human Rights: Michel de la Fournière;
Industries: Jean-Paul Bachy;
Without Portfolio: Roger Fajardie.

In addition to these people the Treasurer of the Party is André Laignel who takes over from Pierre Joxe and there are twelve Assistant Secretaries as follows: Robert Chapuis (Research), Bertrand Delanoë (Press Spokesman), Alain Busnel (Public Sector), Yves Durand and Alain Barrau (Youth), Luc Subré and Pierre Brana (External Relations), Jean Besse and A. Tregouet (Industry), B. Thareau (Agriculture), Martine Buron (Women's Rights), Jacques Huntzinger (International Relations) and Françoise Seligmann (Central Organisation). Each of the areas of policy has a section with staff devoted to it at Party headquarters — the total of people working for the Party is probably around one hundred (though many of these will be part-time).

Effectively Mitterrand has a free hand in deciding what responsibilities individuals will take on and the National Secretariat is assisted by a number of other offices such as the General Delegates, Special Reporters, and National delegates. And the First Secretary has his own highly influential study groups, though these are not constitutional creations.

Additionally there is the Socialist parliamentary group; that is the Assembly and Senate members. Article 19 states that a Deputy must give an understanding to leave parliament should he resign from the Party and II and III give the statutory relationship between Directing Committee and parliamentarians. Thus Article 48 makes it clear that decisions by the Deputies do not commit the Party to policies without assent "even under exceptional circumstances". A little noticed Chapter (III) deals with the case of a clash between Party Directing Committee and Deputies. Article 53 notes that they work together in case of demand from either side (Directorate or Deputies) and in case of conflict (Articles 54, 55 and 56) the two sitting together take binding decisions if 60 per cent decide on an issue. If there is no 60 per cent majority then the Directing Committee decides, but if this should transpire to be a majority for the opposite side of the issue then it must go to a National Convention.

Here is matter for confusion: simple arithmetic could mean that in opposition and in government a moderately unified parliamentary party would swamp the Directing Committee and get its way fairly easily — a fact pointed out (in private) by a Deputy but not the subject of general discussion. In cases where parliament is badly split and the party united then the Directorate would probably prevail but where both are split it is a recipe for chaos. Nobody can say how this would work with the Party in government and until now the Party has been willingly enough dominated by Mitterrand's supporters.

Party candidates are chosen by the Party membership of the constituency in question in both local and national elections but the national party can intervene where an injustice or very serious conflict has taken place. Furthermore the Party candidate for the Presidency is chosen by a National Congress called for the purpose. In 1974 there was no question when François Mitterrand was chosen but the 1969 Congress (which some say was unconstitutional) was a fracas when it chose Defferre as candidate.

FRENCH SOCIALISM AND THE WORKING CLASS[5]

The French Socialist Party is particularly concerned with working class representation within its own ranks and with its own representation on the working class. This is for three principal reasons. First the PS has re-discovered, relative to the defunct SFIO, its sense of 'mission' in the working class and this has been particularly promoted by the currents which entered the new party after 1966 — CERES, Jean Poperen and others. Second the French Socialists are in competition with a Communist Party which has a strong organisational presence in the working class and particularly in the factories. The effects of this were seen during the recent quarrel between Socialist and Communists when, particularly after the failure of the re-negotiation of the common programme in September 1977, the Socialists found that their case was not being properly represented.

Third the French Socialists, unlike the Labour Party, the Spanish Socialists, the German Social Democrats and other big Socialist parties, is not strongly entrenched in trade union politics. This inevitably reduces Socialist influence in working class politics although it has managed to increase its vote in that milieu.

In order to overcome these deficiencies the PS has promoted the workplace section *(section d'enterprise)* in the Party hoping that it will give the Socialists a voice in the working class and bring workers up through the organisation. This is an old idea originally tried by the SFIO as *Groupes sections d'enterprises* immediately after the war and then abandoned because the response was insufficient. At the head of this section until 1979 was Alain Rannou (ex-PSU) and several campaigns have been attempted over the last few years. These included a national campaign against unemployment (summer 1975), a campaign for workers' control (autumn 1975) and a campaign against the freezing of wages (spring 1977). The workplace sections have also been active within the Party putting a view at the Party conferences on industrial matters and in PS study groups.

The workplace section is a constituent part of the Party. That is like the geographical *section* (or ward), it sends delegates to the Federal Congress via the departmental federations. It is therefore the Party organised in the factories, not just Party activists putting the Socialist case in their workplace. The party has hesitated between competing ideas about how to recruit more working class support, though the idea of these sections is particularly defended by CERES. It should also be noted that such workplace sections as do exist are frequently middle class because 'workplace' may very likely mean administration (bank, office or whatever) and because in a factory middle management may be the main Socialist recruiting ground.[6] Hence the paradox that the workplace sections have not been a means to the rapid increase of working class representation in the PS and that even in the sections as a whole the workers (at the widest definition) are a minority. In the Party at Grenoble in 1973 14 per cent were working class delegates (36 per cent were teachers), in the workplace sections 37 per cent were workers (9 per cent teachers). The workplace section is nonetheless important for the French Party.

The "sector for the workplaces" was created at the Epinay Congress of June 1971, largely due to CERES pressure, and Georges Sarre (Deputy, Paris Councillor and CERES) was put in charge. However it was charged that CERES had been taking over the sector and had turned it onto a 'party within a party'. Thus the sector was brusquely attached to the Secretariat for regional Federations (under Louis Mermaz) but with a delegate for the workplace and 'social action'. By 1976 (the Pau Congress) half the Federations claimed to have somebody devoted to 'workplaces' in the leadership. Only three Federations had, however, a full-time member devoted to this function (for the French Party this is small) and the funds for this are, according to CERES, utterly insufficient. Efforts led, though, to the increase of these sections from 400 in 1975 to 1,000 in January 1977 — the PCF has claimed to have, be it noted, 8,000 factory cells.[7]

As might be expected it is traditionally obligatory for the French Socialist activist to join a union but, as might be predicted, Party members do not all join unions. It could be said, in passing, that the SFIO considered an 'organic connection with the unions like the British' but this was rejected, amongst the reasons being that such massive recruitment would lose its class character. French Socialists want to recruit directly within the unions so as to adopt and penetrate a working class group of activists already in a politically engaged area.

Among the other means which the Socialists hope to use to augment the number of workers within its ranks are the progressive tariff, paid posts and schooling. Like most continental Socialist Parties the PS has a membership fee proportional to the income of the activist, workers, peasants, the unemployed etc., thus pay less to join than other people. Paid posts (part-time) are important in making possible worker recruitment and these are very numerous in French

Parties so that, for example, the municipal socialist clubs, Leo-Lagrange have 210 such posts; very few occupants, though are working class. Schooling of the party activists has, for the PS as with the SFIO, along with paid full-time posts, been the main way it has envisaged promoting workers but here again workers have not come forward in large enough numbers to make much difference to the Party's structure. French Communists do not have this problem, these workers are at present at every level of the Party, but that merely highlights the French Socialist dilemma. How can workers be promoted without the PS adopting the authoritarian centralised structure of the PCF? Socialists, therefore, have recognised that there is no answer other than to keep working at the grass roots to recruit more workers. Finally it might be noted that the PS makes a similar effort with the peasants and a huge, and in this case successful, campaign with the young.[8]

CONCLUSION

As can be guessed from this discussion of Socialist organisation, the internal life of the Party is intense and complicated. Yet it should not be assumed that the elaborate machinery established by the Party has guaranteed democracy for the French Socialists. Problems that the SFIO had in the 1950s and 1960s illustrate how this can go wrong. At that time the SFIO remained responsive to a declining band of activists to the neglect of the wider class to whom they should have been responsible. French Socialism's inability to break out of this vicious circle of response to activists and neglect of outside opinion which was in a large part contributory to its decline.

Two other things ought to be remembered when comparing the French Socialists with the Labour Party. The first is that its roots in the working class are nothing like as extensive or as organised as Labours' and secondly the French Socialists are faced with the consistent pressure of the Communists.

Footnotes
1. For an excellent discussion of this subject see John Frears *Political Parties and Elections in the Fifth French Republic,* Charles Hurst, 1977 (Chapter on the Socialist Party).

2. Walter Kendall "Labour Unions in France", *European Community* No.135, June 1970.
3. P.M. Williams, *Crisis and Compromise,* London 1964, deals with the old SFIO on this problem.
4. From P. Bacot Unpublished Thesis University of Lyons.
5. Roland Cayrol "Les militants du Parti Socialiste". *Project,* Sept-Oct, 1974.
6. *Ibid.*
7. *Le Matin,* 16/7/80.
8. *Le Matin,* 12/6/80.

CHAPTER FIVE

The Socialists in Government

by D.S. Bell

The French government elected to carry out the President's programme in June 1981 is a radical one: it is comparable in the scope and intensity of change with the British Labour government of 1945. Mitterrand and Prime Minister Pierre Mauroy have both underlined that the programme is a Socialist one and that it will be carried out with vigour and without respite — whatever the difficulties might be. There is hardly an area of French life which has not been under scrutiny in the Socialist Party during this last ten years and the agenda for change is therefore a long one with wide ramifications although details are yet to be worked out in their entirety.

At a time when the Western world has moved into recession the French Socialists speak a language of optimism and hope and have produced a strategy which runs counter to the main conservative trends which have been visible in Europe and North America since the onset of the recession. Mitterrand has declared that he wants to end unemployment within two years and, with the number of those out of work now over two million in France, this will be very difficult for a new government in a hostile international environment. Nevertheless the Socialists have set themselves this target and relegated inflation to the position of being a secondary enemy (for Giscard, it was the major preoccupation) and they hoped for 3 per cent growth in their first year in government. To attain these ends the Socialists are re-using the old tool of Keynsian reflation to encourage the economy to expand through public spending and through various other acts of state intervention. This strategy will increase the state's role in the French economy to a greater extent than in other Western societies though the Socialists are not unmindful of the implications of this for individual freedoms.

The move towards the collective ownership of the means of production is a centre piece of the new government's programme and the importance placed on nationalisation is shown by the way that it was placed among the first of the major measures to go through parliament in the Autumn of 1981. It was followed by the various parts of the bill to radically decentralise local government as if to emphasise the libertarian aspects of the Socialist programme as much as its collectivisation.

This ensemble of measures is evidence of a determination to bring about an irreversible shift of power and wealth in favour of the least well-off in French Society. Socialists in France would not be content even if they could manage to curb unemployment within their own very tight calendar, they also want to effect a deep-rooted change in the structure of society, to make it more equal and more just. This can be seen more clearly in the detailed measures which the government will be passing during the course of the next years of Mitterrand's presidential term: these will have both an egalitarian and a libertarian impact.

For the Socialist Party the main problems are not the Assembly (where it has a majority) or lack of desire (there is considerable pressure to push the programme through) but rather to operate such a programme in a world which has not so far proved very receptive to Socialist ideas. For example, Mitterrand's call for reflation at the Ottowa heads of state summit did not meet a ready response, nor has the Socialist plan to use Europe as the framework for growth in the 1980s. Nevertheless the government, as Pierre Mauroy made clear in response to the Finance Minister's call for a 'pause', will be pressing ahead and the main social indicators will show whether the French Socialists are nearing their targets, or whether like previous Labour governments, they have been 'blown off course'.

French Socialists have tended to emphasise that their devolution proposals are the 'great affair' of the seven-year term which Mitterrand has at his disposal but there is a long list of reforms and since nationalisation is chronologically the first big measure, and since the concentration is on economics, it would be best to start with these measures before describing power in Socialist France.

NATIONALISATION

The defunct 1972 *Common Programme* which was the manifesto for a joint Communist-Socialist government placed great emphasis on nationalisation and it named the following groups:

Dassault, Roussel-Uclaf, Rhône-Poulenc, ITT-France, Thomson-Brandt, Honeywell-Bull, Pechiney-Ugine-Kuhlmann, Saint-Gobain-Pont-à-Mousson, Compagnie Générale d'Electricité, Usinouf, Wendel-Sidelor, Schneider, Compagnie Francaise de Petroles, plus 36 banks as well as contracting firms and steel (which was added later).

The nationalisations were point 21 of Mitterrand's Presidential programme, they concern the nine industrial groups which have long been on the Left's agenda plus steel (which is in great difficulties in France), arms and space which depend on State finance, and insurance and credit. These make up some 846,000 industrial workers and a turnover of 194 billion francs but there are also the service sectors to be nationalised. All the big banks will be nationalised except foreign banks and some cooperative or local business (Credit agricole, for example). Socialists do not intend to nationalise the various subsidaries or branches of parent companies. The nationalisations were favourably viewed by French public opinion in late 1981 (51 per cent for, 30 per cent against and the rest don't know) despite an arduous battle in the National Assembly when the opposition tabled over 800 amendments. French nationalised industries have, however, traditionally played a different role from the nationalised industries in Britain and companies like Renault have done well since the onset of the OPEC oil crisis (Volkswagen, another nationalised industry, has also had a similar success). At the end of the Second World War de Gaulle himself nationalised a large section of French industry so that the 'inbuilt' opposition to this measure which exists in Britain is to a large extent absent in France. There was a Minister for the 'extension of the public sector', M. Jean Le Garrec, who was to oversee the first *tranche* dealing with the big groups (including almost the entire banking sector). This part of the programme should be finished before 1983. Pierre Mauroy stated that this was intended to give the French economy the boost which it needed.

How these nationalisations are going to work is only slowly becoming clear. Edmond Maire the head of the CFDT (non-Communist) unions in October 1981 criticised the government for 'Stateism', that is the bureaucratisation of these industries rather than their administration through some form of workers' control. In the industries a degree of uncertainty existed so that decisions for the future were not being taken and their exact relation to the State is not yet clear.

Nevertheless the government was moving as rapidly as possible and Mauroy said that there would be no 'lego building' with these groups as if they were toys. Mauroy added that the aim was to free the industries "to take risks and initiatives", which (especially in French banking) capitalist management has made too rare. Secretary of State Le Garrec, who was in charge of the details until the reshuffle of June 1982, made it clear that the groups would play a role within the overall plan to obtain growth, employment, technological development and a world market position. A 'planning contract' for several years will be made with nationalised industries to set the objectives and general lines of growth, i.e. the sectors to be particularly developed, the markets to be conquered and the means to be used with the state making finances available. Nationalised industries will be under the wing of the Minister concerned now that the nationalisation has gone through parliament. Le Garrec has moved from the position overseeing the bill to the Minister dealing with unemployment.

In banking Mauroy stated that competition was to be maintained but that the banks should keep down interest rates, help innovation and to give impetus to weak sectors (which they have not traditionally done).

A restructured public sector is expected by the government to play a 'locomotive role' in the economy with a general coherent plan. In contrast to private industry, public industry can take a long-term view and thus adapt to a rapidly changing world but the Socialists have talked in terms of 're-conquering' the French market which will in turn enable export development. Small industries will also, it is stated, be helped by the attitude of the new public sector towards them (and especially on loans and credit).

Nationalisations are not a complete take-over by the state of French industry: when the nationalisation is completed the percentage of the GNP from public industry will be only 16 per cent. Socialists want to maintain a market economy intact, though they wish to guide the market and to limit its excesses. Nationalised industries will play a role in this, as they will in reviving the French economy, but they are part of an overall economic strategy of reflation.

SOCIALIST ECONOMICS

The general Socialist approach is to attack the roots of the current French malaise. This, they state, is the inequality of French society which exacerbates the class struggle and causes workers to press for higher wages. Wage demands (provoked by inequalities) cause firms to put up prices to keep the profit rate high and these are in turn transmitted into higher prices which cause further wage pressure and so on in increasingly vicious circles. Socialist egalitarian measures are meant to cut into this spiral. Reduction of structural inequalities is thus at the heart of the Socialist economic strategy as is the need to counter rising prices, and increase the living standards of the poorest.

Socialists have envisaged the problems of an 'investment strike' by business although no specific measures have been designed to deal with this. Costs were reduced for small business but before the four month freeze of July 1982 in main the effort was one of persuasion mainly evidenced by Prime Minister Pierre Mauroy's *tour de France* to persuade business to invest, expand and take on workers. But the President has also been concerned not to undermine business 'confidence' too much and Jacques Delors — Finance Minister — has been particularly worried about the impact of Socialist measures on the business community — so far he has been overridden. The main point about Socialist relations with business is that the government will not allow business fears to restrain the drive for reform although they need investment and the elusive 'business confidence'.

Socialists in France have emphasised the importance of the Plan in the economy and they have determined to restore the Plan to its rightful place. One of the first measures of the Mauroy government was to establish a mini-Plan in the interim between the drawing up of a Five-Year Plan in 1984 and breaking with the preceding Giscard Plans. Michel Rocard, Minister of the Plan, outlined a policy which would work to increase economic demand, improve competitivity so that the interior (French) market could be 'reconquered' and through expansion work to reduce unemployment. For the government the Plan is intended to orient investment so as to allow the market to play an adjusting role and it establishes a coherent economic policy, especially with the pivotal aid of the nationalised sector.

The interim mini-Plan sets out the objectives of the government in economics. These are: to create 400,000 to 500,000 new jobs in two years, to introduce the 35-hour week by 1985, to increase family allowances by 50 per cent, to increase family purchasing power by 2 per cent annually, to maintain the average purchasing power of wages, to increase the minimum wage regularly, to increase from 1.9 per cent to 2.5 per cent the national outlay on research, the construction of 405,000 new houses in 1982, the stabilisation of the various taxes and business charges, an energy target of 232 million tons (petrol equivalent) and a 3 per cent growth rate from 1981-1983.

French National Assembly deputies voted this interim Plan in mid-December 1981: during the debate Rocard defended a number of Socialist concepts including the use of the public sector as a 'vector' of the government's economic strategy with the nationalised banks being used to help industry to expand. In Rocard's concept the Plan is the act of the whole government and is consequently binding on the government, but it is also the result of numerous bargains between Ministers and between social groups. For the future the Plan will be much more a work of consensus and consultation than was the hasty interim Plan. In particular regional consultation will be developed as will the statistical office for planning and in particular the various social forces will be brought into the process of working out future economic development.

The attempt to introduce justice into the working of the economic system is exemplified by the creation of the Ministry of Solidarity now headed by Bérégovoy who took over in June 1982 from Nicole Questiaux. This Ministry will bring together everything which touches the social services, family allowances, unemployment, state benefits as well as equality at work and the shortening of the working week. In addition to these measures to help the least well off there have been taxation measures to redistribute income. A wealth tax was introduced in the 1982 budget which will concern, for the most part, land and housing but which should bring in 5-8 billion francs.

In the housing market Socialists intend to remove the abuses of the last few years — something conceded by Mitterrand during the election campaign — by re-establishing rent control, security of tenure, and switching resources to HLM (council housing) for the lower paid. In particular the Socialist government has set itself the aim of building 450,000 to 500,000 per year (especially HLM) to stem the falling rate of housing construction which has even hit the private sector. This sector of the government's programme will be crucial since the building industry is intended to be a spearhead for subsequent economic expansion and job creation. By controlling land sales more closely the Socialists hope to end the general liberation in this section but not quality or choice.

François Mitterrand has taken a particularly close interest in the key industrial sector for the future, i.e. technology, electronics and computers. Research in these areas is to be stepped up in the hope that 'sunrise' industries will produce a 'silicon valley' effect in France. Particular emphasis was put on this research and advanced technology sector after the second devaluation and the control of industry was also transferred to J.P. Chevènement. Investment in research is to increase by 80 billion francs to 2.5 per cent of GNP by 1985 and the Minister of Research J.P. Chevènement (of CERES) is to divert funds through the agency of the state on to the future 'winners' and an open debate is being organised on research priorities inside the research community. For the new Socialist government the hope is that industrial take-off will occur in six areas: bio-technology, energy, electronics, robotics, employment and co-operation with the Third World. Since the President's personal interest in this area is close it can be expected to develop but it is also where Socialists expect expansion to come from.

REFLATION IN ONE COUNTRY

The French Socialist government was forced to devalue the franc in the autumn of 1981 and again in 1982. The devaluation of 1981 could be explained as the legacy of the Giscard-Barre government which had kept the franc over-valued as a way of keeping inflation down. However, the second devaluation was more complicated and forced a re-thinking of the government's strategy. Although the Socialist government had managed to stimulate business slightly and to keep the number of unemployed from rising: the unpalatable facts were that interest rates were high, the balance of payments not good, and inflation though not rising, was way ahead of its principal trading partners (i.e. 14 per cent as against that of 5 per cent in West Germany). Commentators therefore began to talk about "U-turns" and reversals, as the Socialist government imposed a four month wages and prices freeze, as several Ministers were reshuffled, as the government called for economic 'rigour' and introduced an emergency budget in autumn 1982 to control spending.

Pierre Mauroy talked about the need to keep the budget deficit to 3 per cent and, in a clear signal that the government had decided not to allow spending to spiral, the new Minister of Solidarity, Bérégouoy, stated that he would try to cut the social security deficit. He departed from Questiaux's view that "I am a minister of reform: not a minister of accounts", by stating that he knew "how to count". Essentially this meant bringing other groups into the category of those who have to pay to the unemployment fund (civil servants were included soon after his appointment). The social security budget remains a problem for it is financed from wage earner and business contributions and is separate from the rest of the budget.

Apart from controlling government spending the move towards a prices and incomes policy is another innovation. The four month freeze was intended to break inflationary expectations and the possibility that this could be extended was left open. But the French Socialists will be faced with difficulties in trying to impose an incomes policy: the Communist CGT unions and the PCF immediately declared themselves hostile to the wages freeze and unrest in French industry means that they will be in the front line of the government's attempt to make a norm stick. "Austerity", or as the Socialists prefer to say 'rigour', has not been popular on the Left and although they could be proposing restrained growth of income and not a fall in the standard of living there is very little room for manoeuvre in a gloomy world environment.

Yet the restrictions on the growth of government spending and the freeze do not tell the whole story. French Socialists have decided that the single pronged attack on unemployment had to be replaced by a double pronged attack on both inflation and unemployment. The aim of reducing unemployment has not been abandoned nor has the intention to run a budget deficit and to stimulate growth through reflation, but the Socialists have decided that attention must be given to inflation otherwise the competitive position of French industry could be undermined or devaluations could become increasingly desperate. In broad terms the government decided that reflation would go ahead but that inflation was a more serious problem than had been granted before the second devaluation of June 1982.

If French Socialists were still betting on a Keynesian answer to unemployment they had not abandoned their feel for state intervention. In a major part of the reshuffle after devaluation J.P. Chevénement was given the Industry Ministry (in succession to Pierre Dreyfus) in addition to the Research and Technology Ministry which he already ran. Chevènement would run a French equivalent to the Japanese Ministry of International Trade and Industry, a super-Ministry which will reactivate French industry on the basis of modern technology. The Research budget will be increased by about 18 per cent from 1983-1985 (to become about 2.5 per cent of GNP) but Chevènement will also be developing finance for industry and searching out markets and trade. It is on Chevènement that the responsibility falls for working out the direction for the new nationalised industries and, in particular, for developing the steel industry before the fateful date of 1986 when EEC decisions will intervene. Chevènement's view was characteristically blunt when he declared that nothing less than the future of France was at stake in an economic war for survival. There was, as could have been predicted, a tension between the interventionist and forceful side of socialism and the more cautious approach of the Party's financial experts and of those who were worried about inflation and tempted to control the money supply.

HUMAN RIGHTS

One of the first acts which Mitterrand took as president was to invoke clemency for a condemned murderer and the abolition of capital punishment followed quickly. French Socialists are particularly insistent on the human rights aspect of their programme, a desire which was underlined by the appointment of Robert Badinter as Justice Minister. The "New citizenship" of Socialist France in Pierre Mauroy's phrase, involves the extension of justice, the repeal of several much disliked laws and immigrant rights. Thus Peyrefitte's 'Security and Liberty' law which became a symbol of repressive law for the Left has been practically abolished.

Apart from the Peyrefitte law (which was attacked by the Ecologists as well), Mitterrand promised that judicial independence would be ensured, that there would be a prison amnesty (6,235 people were released) and that 'exceptional' measures would be ended. The *Cour de sûreté de l'Etat* was criticised by Mitterrand on its inauguration in 1963 as "unjustifiable in its rules and condemnable in its errors" and in July the Assembly and Senate abolished it so that these matters will now go before ordinary assizes courts. Under Peyrefitte the French prison population expanded to 40,000 places by 33 per cent in two years, and by 1 August this was down to 31,500, because in addition to the usual but generous categories of amnesty there were the liberations of breakers of press law, permit breakers, those accused of state security infringements and imprisoned trade unionists but many 'white collar crimes' were not amnestied. These generosities were not popular with public opinion.

It will take a good two years to see many of these good intentions become statute because the process of writing laws is a slow one and even the Peyrefitte law cannot be simply repealed — the penal parts will be abolished dealing with habitual criminals, remission and penalties but the code of procedure will have to be re-written by the constituted Leaute committee. There is also a public relations aspect which, the Minister has noted, is difficult in an atmosphere worsened by the propaganda for the Peyrefitte laws.

Likewise François Autain, the Minister for Immigrant Workers, does not have a very big margin of manoeuvre, but he nevertheless wants to end the twilight world of the immigrant laws. This means regularising the position of many immigrants (i.e. for some 300,000 workers) although there will be no vote for immigrants in the 1983 local elections as was once expected and the customs measures on immigration have been tightened.

There are three principal measures in view in this particular area: the clandestinity of current illegal immigrants will be ended, the number of entry visas will be restricted, except for families (the PS was against any further immigration) and the problem of immigration (schools, culture etc.) will be examined with the relevant home country. The government has already stopped arrests and expulsions, prolonged permits to stay and regularised the status of some. However, there was an increased battle against the black market in workers after the turn of 1981 but the government will help professional training. Moreover local government will be asked to make proposals and the State will aid their plans (by signing contracts) with more money. Second generation 'immigrants' are a particular subject of concern — as for the immigrant vote, the storm released by Foreign Minister Cheysson's remarks on the subject in Algeria show the delicacy of this problem, and it is no longer on the agenda.

François Mitterrand's desire for a 'great single and lay' education system is the outcome of a major programme albeit one which evokes all the old-style clashes over clericalism in the past. Education Minister Alain Savary is, however, pursuing his 'consensus' strategy to eliminate state-aided private education in the long term but not the 'plurality' of schools. State aid to such private institutions will not, then, be abruptly withdrawn and the state service will be expanded before any attempt is made to integrate all schools.

Since this is mainly an issue of Church schools it is worth noting that the Church and the Catholic parents' association are not making a 'school war' out of it but negotiations have not yet started on this issue. Within education the morale of the teachers seems to be particularly low and amongst the first measures Mauroy took were the revocation of the April 2 circular and the unfreezing of posts. With the creation of education priority zones the target of one teacher to twenty-five will be pursued, but deprived areas will get more. For teachers the Ministry has announced the re-employment of all this year's auxiliary teachers and university assistants awaiting tenure. Reforms of recruitment and teacher training are in the pipeline and the 'Sauvage' University laws which restricted representation have been repealed. But numerous rectors (heads of education in regions) have been replaced (about 27) in the hope of 'depoliticising' the education institutions. Given the current ferment in French education, the pressures for reform, and the large number of interested pressure groups, the Ministry under Alain Savary will have a long consultation process to go through.

It can, of course, be assumed that like education, culture features highly amongst the preoccupations of any French Socialist government and the Socialist Minister Jack Lang has taken this symbolic sector in hand along with an unprecedented increase in the budget and a forceful decentralisation. The increase in funds will serve to loosen up the situation, particularly in disfavoured regions, which will allow career prospects to open again. In the decentralisation laws, article 61 will devolve the responsibility of local government will be lightened in certain current expenditures (museums, libraries, art schools etc.).

A change inside the Ministry of Culture will end the administrative functional isolation of different sectors which it is hoped will recreate initiative inside the organisation. In the cinema and book industries the new Ministry looks to the nationalised banks to restart investment for commercial reasons. Giscard's 19th century museum has been given a new head which will change its function and the Villette will be transformed into a popular musical centre for dance, opera, etc). (Much has changed since its original inception.) A Franco-Latin Academy will be set up (as under foreign policy initiatives) and this will increase the Third World impact of French culture. In general the cultural sector will be one of Socialist action to decentralise initiative and increase cultural exchange in the perspective of changing the *cadre de vie* or lifestyle of the general French population. It is the first time in many years that France has actually had a policy for culture and it is a sector of particular concern to the president.

DECENTRALISATION

France is a notoriously centralised system. The French Left with its Jacobin tradition has long been in favour of this emphasis of the role of the state but times have changed. Self-management *(autogestion)* has been a major theme of the thinking of the new Socialist Party so that Interior Minister Defferre's decentralisation proposals are inspired by this new spirit. It is, of course, very much a French reform because some of the procedures are adaptation (or abolitions) of the pre-existing institutions. Nevertheless, the reforms go much further than the Scottish and Welsh devolution measures would have gone had they been put into effect in Britain.

So far only part of the decentralisation law has been worked out and passed and the main part, concerning finances and levels of responsibility have not yet been drafted. Yet the face of French local government has already been changed, for the most part irreversibly. Gone are the 'Prefects', the state appointed guardians, approvers, and initiators of all local government action. Prior to November 1981 local councils, mayors and departments had to submit their plans, budgets and works for the approval of these officials who would often refer them up to Paris or veto them. 'Prefects' have been replaced by Republican *Commissaires* who will have certain powers to investigate local government if something appears to have been done illegally, budgets will be referred to special audit courts, and local authorities will be able to raise loans although exactly what powers of taxation they will have has not yet been decided (it should be before the 1983 local elections).

It is intended to create directly elected regional Assemblies and Prefectoral authority over the Department (county council) has been removed. Corsica has been given its own elected Assembly, the Basques will probably get a Department of their own, as will the Bretons, and Paris may have a special system of local government; all these innovations run counter to the idea that the French Republic is 'one and indivisible'.

FOREIGN POLICY AND DEFENCE

Foreign policy is traditionally a presidential area of action in the Fifth Republic and it remains so under the leadership of François Mitterrand although policy is in line with the philosophy worked out in opposition. Here too there have been considerable changes from previous Right-wing regimes through the policies are not necessarily in line with those of the British Left.

Mitterrand has tended to emphasise the disagreements with Moscow (the only major capital not yet visited by the president) over such issues as Afghanistan, Poland and human rights and the Socialist government have supported the American Cruise/Pershing programme of emplacements in Europe and have increased their own nuclear weapons programme to build a seventh nuclear submarine and a neutron bomb. Unilateralism in France is very weak and supported neither by the Socialist Left (CERES) nor the CPF.

However Mitterrand has also made clear his differences with Reagan and American policy. France under the Socialists will not accept that dictatorships in Latin America should be supported just because they are 'anti-Communist' and 'progressive' movements overthrowing military rulers are not inevitably to be viewed with suspicion. In arms sales, which are a major export industry in France, the government intends to alter the policy of selling to anybody who will buy and will not sell arms to obnoxious regimes.

As an extension of this concern the French government intends to increase aid to the Third World and to re-orient its policies to under-developed states (there will also be a cultural programme for the Third World). France under the Socialists has also called for new European initiatives on North-South policy although this has gone in hand with a series of policy proposals intended to re-animate the European community.

In sum, therefore, Socialist foreign policy is one of firmness on human rights issues and of diplomatic initiative in certain favoured areas such as Central America or Europe. The French Socialists intend to break with the cynical 'national interest' policies of the Fifth Republic's previous governments and show that there is a moral dimension — running *sometimes* against pure self-interest — in France's new foreign policy.

CONCLUSION

French Socialists have started an experiment which has implications for the rest of Europe and which is the mirror image of the Thatcher-Howe approach: out of the window has gone 'sado-monetarism' as the government of France goes for growth through consumption, deficit finance, increased production and reflation. Mitterrand's programe sets a precedent for Labour in 1981 (with unemployment and inflation at high levels in both societies) by using the tool of state intervention within the context of levelling measures designed to egalitarianise society.

Mitterrand, in the 9 December 1981 presidential statement not only underlined the 'return to growth' but also stated that this is a Socialist approach between social-democracy and Stalinism. This is indeed how French Socialists see their own action, they are, in the words of the *Projet Socialiste* "not reforming capitalism but breaking with it". According to the PS, Sweden, which has not nationalised the major businesses, is not 'Socialist' despite its redistributionist policies because it has not touched the central institutions of capitalism. France is now going along the path of increased redistribution and further social expenditures both of which are supported by theory and run counter to the general European trend.

The French Socialist programme is to build a more humane society as Socialist leaders have stated "the law of the capitalist system is the law of the jungle and the jungle belongs to the strongest and if the strongest escapes from the necessity to eat the weakest, then they are the weakest and they will be eaten" (quote from *La Rose au Poing*). The principal behind these actions, as it is behind the decentralisation proposals, is to re-animate collective decisions by giving power back to the people and restricting the market to a more limited (though still extant) role. The Socialist leaders have stated, on this point, that "a population has needs which risk being unsatisfied through the single mechanism of the market". (Primary needs must be cared for.)

POWER IN SOCIALIST FRANCE

One of the persistent debates in the British Left is about how to get a programme efficiently carried out and how to ensure ministerial control over civil servants. The problem does not appear in the same way in debates on the French Left and the purpose of this section is to explain why with a brief look at the structure of power in Socialist France.

Unlike Britain the French government has the power to nominate its own private office (which is not preponderantly composed of civil servants) and to change the heads of the various state organisations to ensure the application of its policies. There is therefore a complete re-staffing of private offices which are quite numerous (38 in the Elysee and 44 in Matignon for the president and PM respectively) and outside experts are drafted in. Unlike previous Fifth Republic regimes the Socialists have not inherited people from the outgoing government and they have not been so dependent on the graduates of the elite schools and they are, of course, mostly Socialists and many are personally close to their Minister.

THE PRESIDENT

Presidentialism is now an established feature of the Fifth Republic although it is not a constitutional creation and was for a long time fought by the Left. The President does not, however, interfere in day-to-day administration — which is the Prime Minister's business — but lays down the general lines of policy to be carried out by the government. Presidents have, however, taken particular interest in certain portfolios. Naturally, foreign affairs and defence have been presidential areas but Mitterrand is also interested in culture and in research in technology and electronics. Even here there is a split responsibility with the Prime Minister (who went, for example to Poland on a foreign policy mission) and the staff of the Elysée do not intervene in government as active agents.

In fact the Elysée staff is too small to do other than monitor the work of the government so that the President knows whether the programme is being applied and what problems there are. The Elysée general secretary has responsibility for the general running of the President's aides through the *cabinet* (private office) under Andre Rousselet and J.C. Colliard organises the administration. In addition there is the special councillor Jacques Attali (who is not one of the shrinking violets of the Elysée) and twelve technical councillors with other associates who include Regis Debray.

(i) The President and Prime Minister

Giscard d'Estaing's presidentialism was proverbial: this extended from the trivial (getting himself served first at dinner) to the political (interference in detailed policy). Giscard seems to have started by sending long detailed messages to individual Ministers about policy and even quite specific measures cutting out the Prime Minister. Relations between Giscard and Chirac fell into this mould although those between Giscard and Barre were less detrimental to the Prime Minister. In the Giscard/Barre era Giscard seems to have kept the PM informed of policy decisions.

It must be noted that this is *not* a relationship determined by the Constitution: the political pre-eminence of the President is due to his position as leader of the majority in the Assembly. The president has no *de jure* powers (except the two-edged power to dissolve the Assembly in Article 12) his powers are *de facto* based on the political domination of the majority — this has not changed, Mitterrand dominates the Socialist Party.

This said, Mitterrand has moved to what could be called a distinctly 'Gaullist' position on the institutions. Thus the Elysée is not, as it was under Giscard, the powerhouse of government, this is the Prime Minister's role. Mitterrand's programme includes the '110 propositions' and Mitterrand's campaign commitments, but the implementation, the details, and the mode of operation are determined by Mauroy. Moreover the President does not interfere in the day-to-day running of government, this is Mauroy's task, and political demands pass through the PM not the Elysée. Unfortunately this has not prevented either surprise announcements of policy being sprung on the Matignon (like the ill-advised plan to reform Paris local government) or quarrels between ministers breaking out from time to time.

There is one area where Mitterrand is very active: Foreign policy. Here the old Gaullist idea of the *domaine reservé* appears to be appropriate. Mitterrand is very concerned about foreign affairs (economics by contrast, is not his forte). As mentioned, the staff at the Elyslèe is not large enough to control the government, but there are times when a particular policy is of special interest to Mitterrand and in these cases an aide of the President sits in on the deliberations. Likewise relations with the parliament pass through the Prime Minister and not through the Elysée although the President does regularly (2-3 times/week) meet the head of the Socialist Party, Lionel Jospin — this is crucial because Mitterrand still remains close to the business of the PS which is his power base.

Mitterrand, it may seem, is because of the Assembly majority of Socialists a more powerful President than Giscard but this is not in practice the case. To start with the relations between Mauroy and Mitterrand are close and problems are settled between them during their meetings, not behind the PM's back. A regular 'working breakfast' has been instituted for President and PM to iron out the issues for the day's Cabinet meetings. Things are not usually 'sprung on' the Prime Minister nor does the Prime Minister allow an institutional tension to develop between Matignon (the French 'No.10') and the Elysée. The slow reconcilation of Mauroy and Mitterrand since Metz provides the dominant political axis for the new government: things revolve around that. This relationship is more like de Gaulle/Pompidou than the Giscard/Chirac years.

Cabinet meetings resemble more the British Cabinet than they do the Giscard Cabinet pattern (c.f. Françoise Giroud's *le comedie du pouvoir* in which Giscard's hortatory and aloof style is mercilessly portrayed). There are Cabinet meetings on Wednesday mornings attended by all Ministers and all Secretaries of State. These meetings are discussions around the table but are not followed by a vote, they are chaired by the President and the discussion is terminated by the Prime Minister.

Thus for example, an energy policy discussion was opened by Minister for Research J.P. Chevènement and closed by Mauroy. However the major disagreements are settled in inter-ministerial committees between departments before they reach the Cabinet. This is a Socialist innovation; Giscard centralised affairs to pass through the Elysée, the inter-Ministerial committees devolve on the PM (see below). Cabinet minutes and its agenda as in the UK are prepared by a permanent civil servant and this is perhaps one of the few politically sensitive posts filled from the permanent establishment which means that, although key, it is not quite so powerful as in the UK. The *Secretaire Général du Government* liaises bewtween Mauroy and Mitterrand on the Cabinet agenda and other matters.

(ii) The PM's Office

The contrast between Britain and France could not be greater in organisational terms. In France the system of the Ministerial *'cabinet'* had evolved long before the Fifth Republic: in this system politicians in government bring with them a group of aides who act as a private office. (In Britain this would be done by permanent civil servants). It would not be possible to develop such extensive political control over the detailed policy needed to carry out the government programme or to co-ordinate such policies without such a (by British standards) huge technical/political service.

There are about 44 people in the Prime Minister's office *(Cabinet)* plus a military *cabinet* and a *Senator en Mission aupres du PM* (M. Pontillon). There is a split between the political and party apparatus which is headed by Mm. Pontillon as *Chef du Secretariat particulier* and which deals with such matters as speeches, visits, lobbyists etc. and the government office.

This office has its HQ in the Matignon and there is a Conseileur Technique to deal with the business of the major Ministries (Transport, Social, Culture etc.) and within that a smaller group with a Charge de Mission who prepares the PM's dossier on these subjects. In this way the PM keeps an eye on what Ministries are doing and what needs to be co-ordinated between Ministries. Inter-Ministerial problems are worked out by the technical *cabinet* before they go to Mauroy but if there is disagreement he may then step in to resolve the difficulty.

The President, despite the existence of a similar smaller staff, is not involved. As a footnote it could be mentioned that the four Communists are exemplary Ministers and function with in this system: like other Ministers they have their *cabinet* which includes a few non-Communists.

Schematically the system looks something like this.

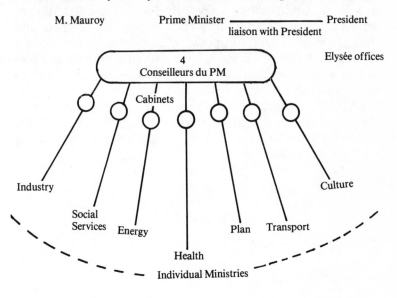

(iii) The Parliamentary Group

The Socialist Party has a majority in the Assembly alone but Party/Government relations are the responsibility of a 'whip' M.A. Labariere. Meetings are called with the group where policy is discussed but, unlike the previous Presidential practice, the Prime Minister often participates in such sessions: Mauroy is rather like Michael Foot in his attachment to parliament. Mauroy is therefore in close contact with the parliamentary group (which is considerably to his taste) and with party spokesmen. For example, again on energy, Paul Quilès gave considerable advice to Mauroy, indeed advice is given on all subjects very frequently.

The Socialist group is much more complicated and has a life of its own. Since the government has decided not to use the closure as Giscard did there is a much more sensitive parliament/PM relationship. As could be expected the Socialist group has an independent existence and has asserted its independence at times: in parenthesis it could be noted that so far this assertion of independence has not been along the usual lines of Party currents. Thus the Socialist group opposed the government on the issue of advertising on the new local radio stations (they were for and the government were against) and eventually a compromise was reached, and the Socialist group opposed the government on its immigration policy and caused it to adopt a more liberal text in line with its commitments in opposition. It is too early to say whether the Assembly will develop a new role itself — as the Socialist programme would lead to expect — because it takes two to evolve a consensus and the parties of the Right refused to enter into this 'game'. It may yet develop, though it seems unlikely.

PART TWO: CERES

by David Hanley

CHAPTER ONE

CERES* — An Open Conspiracy?

THE ORIGINS AND DEVELOPMENT OF CERES
The earliest recognisable origins of the *Centre d'études, de recherche et d'éducation socialiste* probably go back to 1964, when its founders joined the then French Socialist Party SFIO. The most significant members of the group were those acknowledged today as its leaders, viz. Jean-Pierre Chevènement and Didier Motchane, and Chevènement has described their state of mind at this time.[1] Their formative years had seen the collapse of the Fourth Republic, largely as a result of the colonial war in Algeria, and the consequent imposition of Gaullism. By the mid-60s these young men already had a clear analysis of the workings of French capitalism and its relationship to the international economic environment. They were also aware of the real political and social fragility of the apparently stable Gaullist edifice; consequently they held that the prospects for a revival of French Socialism were, despite appearances, strong. What is significant, however, is that they chose to situate their action inside the old SFIO, although in 1964 that Party seemed the last place for energetic activists with new ideas, because it had been in steady and apparently irreversible decline since its peak of 350,000 members and 23 per cent of the popular vote in 1945, when it shared power with Communists and Christian Democrats and laid the bases for the post-war modernisation of French capitalism along welfare state lines.

By 1964 SFIO was reaping the rewards for its increasing political compromises with French conservatism. In the war which French governments fought against Algerian nationalism from 1954 onwards, it had when in office been unable to effect either a military or a negotiated solution. Rather it had, especially during the Guy Mollet government of 1956-7, increased military expenditure and repression in

*Centre d'Etudes de Récherches et d'Education Socialistes.

Algeria to unheard-of lengths and dealt extremely harshly
with domestic opposition to its Algerian policy. The weakness of Mollet and his colleagues also contributed greatly to
that progressive abandoning of government authority to the
soldier/settler alliance in Algiers that would eventually dig
the grave of the Fourth Republic. In 1958, when de Gaulle
was installed at the head of the new Fifth Republic, the
Mollet group helped legitimise his rule by accepting posts in
his transitional governments. SFIO might thus have seemed
redundant as a political force, because on the one hand the
Communist Party (PCF) showed no appreciable signs of
withering away; whilst on the other, numerous socialists and
progressives were turning away from SFIO, either towards
the new united Socialist Party (PSU), which aimed to group
the non-communist left into a new, principled socialist party
or, less ambitiously, towards the political clubs — small
groups of a rather intellectual, indeed 'technocratic' nature,
who thought in terms of a modernizing strategy, pivoting in
practice on some sort of centre-left alliance. Such an alliance
would bring together the SFIO, some other small groups
from the non-Communist Left and what by then remained of
the centre in French politics, i.e. the rumps of Radicalism and
Christian Democracy. These currents might, together
perhaps with some of the more progressive elements of the
moderate Right, combine on a programme of economic
expansion and a certain amount of social reform. The
Communist Party would be firmly shut out of such an
alliance, though the votes of its supporters on the second
ballot would be welcomed — and indeed expected if this
strategy were to work. But the unsuccessful attempt of
Gaston Defferre to start up a presidential campaign in 1964
on just such a ticket showed that this type of alliance is harder
to put together than might first seem apparent. Eventually
most of these people would find their way into the new
Socialist Party (PS) at various times after 1969; but the
CERES group began and remained in SFIO — a gesture
which in 1964 might have seemed symptomatic of some kind
of death-wish.

In fact the group's gamble was based on a number of
considerations which in retrospect seem to have been
remarkably far-sighted. Leaving aside a certain 'workerist'

(ouvriériste)[2] nostalgia and a sentimental attachment to the
SFIO for its past achievements and the weight of its traditions
(and this type of consideration is an important part of the
make-up of many CERES activists), there were sound
reasons for choosing SFIO. It still had, despite its decline,
something of a popular base, with a bedrock of electoral
support and extensive implantation in local government plus
a presence within the labour and co-operative movements. In
fact, apart from the PCF, still too Stalinist to be considered
seriously as a force for social change, SFIO was for all its
imperfections the only really structured popular
organisation. It thus made sense for Socialists with ideas to
try and revive it from within, rather than attempt laboriously
to create an alternative. It is in this pragmatic spirit that
CERES began its work, and its long-term aim was fixed from
the start[3]:

> . . . to advance towards a mass, class-based Party. CERES is only a means
> for transforming the Party.

CERES has always proclaimed that its ultimate ambition
was to disappear, once having achieved its aim of
transforming the Party. But in practice it was never likely to
be so simple. For any attempt to revive SFIO from within
meant a struggle against the existing leadership, at the very
least so as to impose policy changes upon it or, most
logically, to supplant it. CERES wanted to capture the Party
from within and hence was always likely to be 'a party within
a party' or in H.G. Wells' phrase, 'an open conspiracy'. Just
how apparent this was to the founders is not clear; but in the
years after 1966 CERES increasingly took on this sort of
profile. It would seem that the group has gone about as far as
possible today in developing its own identity and autonomous
action while still remaining inside the PS; and in conclusion
this chapter will attempt to say how the group might develop.
For the moment, though, the main steps in CERES' itinerary
since 1964 will be outlined.

CERES first began to express itself as an organised group
in 1966. Publishing material either in sympathetic journals
(e.g. the now defunct *Combat)* or on its own account, its
main efforts were propagandist rather than organisational.
As befitted a group consisting mainly of intellectuals, it

sought to act as a 'think tank', hoping to influence SFIO to adopt new policies, either by the above publications or in papers submitted to Guy Mollet, then head of SFIO and personally sympathetic to the group (doubtless because he was unaware of its long term aims). CERES also began to organise a series of seminars through 1967 and 1968, which drew considerable publicity, especially the one on industrial policy in April 1968. At this early stage many typical CERES themes are already evident: the need to transform the Socialist Party, with stress laid on its role as educator and raiser of consciousness: the necessity of a full alliance with the PCF including a Common Programme of Government (CPG) as the only means of achieving social change in France: bitter attacks on any modernising strategy based on a Centre-Left or 'third force' alliance (i.e. excluding the PCF): mistrust of the EEC, the Atlantic alliance and US hegemony. Full commitment to workers' control seems only to have come after May 1968. At the same time, CERES took on some organisational density. The arrival of Georges Sarre, a key figure in the postal workers' union in Paris, brought a number of union activists into the group and gave it the beginnings of a wider base among wage-earners; by 1969 CERES would thus be able to win control of the Party's Paris federation. By 1968 the Paris federation was in fact badly run down. The activity of Chevènement and his friends in the fourteenth *arrondissement* (where many of Sarre's postal workers were located in big sorting offices) was the springboard for revival. Under Sarre's energetic secretaryship the first socialist workplace branches were set up (in the post office and broadcasting services): talks were begun with the local Communist federation and several joint protest actions undertaken: the possibility of a common programme of government was even discussed, much to the annoyance of the then Socialist Party leader, A. Savary. At the same time CERES influence was beginning to spread from Paris out into the provinces; largely, it would seem, as a result of personal contacts made within various Party bodies, and the effects of CERES journalism and propaganda, like-minded groups were beginning to emerge. Thus by late 1968 the Savoie federation under G. Antonin would have a CERES majority at its head.

The 'events' of May 1968 seem to have confirmed, on the level of theory, the CERES view that what it termed the electorialism of SFIO was an inadequate basis on which to challenge modern capitalism. CERES felt that SFIO placed exclusive reliance on winning a parliamentary majority, as the means of bringing in socialism by decree; in so doing it neglected the possibilities of the various mass-movements increasingly likely to emerge in contemporary societies. Also the 'events' concentrated CERES reflection on the possibility of a new model of self-managing socialism *(autogestion),* of which some analyses see the events of May as a herald. On the level of political organisation, however, the events opened up a crisis within the French Left that would give CERES an unhoped-for chance to exert influence.

It will be recalled that as a result of tension generated by different responses to the events the electoral alliance of SFIO, clubs and Radicals fell apart; at the same time the reconciliation between these partners and the Communists was also interrupted drastically, not least by the Soviet invasion of Czechoslovakia. In these circumstances SFIO decided to rebuild itself completely; this process would take until June 1971, when at its Epinay congress, the new Party (which now became the Parti Socialiste) took on the shape that has characterised it since, under the leadership of F. Mitterrand. What happened during the years before the Epinay Congress was that among all the factions of SFIO and other left-wingers that eventually joined together into the new Party CERES held a crucial balancing position. This it used to the full so as to imbue the new Party with policy and organisational inputs that were very much its own.

The Epinay Congress saw a struggle for control of the new Party between different factions of SFIO and newcomers. The Mauroy-Defferre group, which spoke for the biggest federations of the old SFIO, wanted to see the Party revived, but still thought at heart of involving it in a Centre/Left alliance. The Mollet-Savary group were above all fearful of getting drawn into some kind of binding deal with the Communists, and they were joined for purposes of this congress by the small group around J. Poperen (usually more favourable to an aliance with the PCF, though subject to strict conditions): together they commanded 46 per cent of delegate votes. Now Mauroy and Defferre were ready, for their part, to vote with Mitterrand's supporters, for their anxiety to revive the party outweighed such reservations as they had about Mitterrand (i.e. that he was new to socialism and that he was reputedly keener than they on a pact with the PCF). But even this alliance only yielded 45 per cent. CERES thus stood in the unlikely position of kingmaker, as it had 8½ per cent of the votes. The group used its strength to the full, allying with the Mitterrandists and Mauroy-Defferre (whom they had denounced prior to the congress as the 'real Right', in contrast to the Molletists who were merely the 'fake Left'!) This alliance of strange bedfellows was nonetheless highly advantageous to CERES; the PS adopted for its leadership bodies the system of proportional representation, whereby supporters of any motion at the Party congress must be represented on the *comité directeur* and *bureau executif* in proportion to the number of votes obtained by their motion (above a 5 per cent threshold). CERES and Mitterrand also obtained a firm commitment to the alliance with the PCF, based on a proper common programme, and an undertaking that the new Party programme would be on the lines of *autogestion* (Chevènement was to be one of the main authors of the eventual 1972 document). Henceforth CERES was indeed represented on the national bodies of the PS, including the secretariat (a virtual shadow cabinet inside the *bureau executif* and the main locus of decision making at the top of the PS), with Sarre the secretary in charge of socialist workplace branches.

CERES strength swelled to 20 per cent of the delegate vote at the Grenoble conference of 1973 and to 25.4 per cent at Pau in 1975 (i.e. by now the group could claim to speak for some 35,000 members, compared with a few hundreds in 1968 and some twenty in 1966). Further policy successes had ensured during this time, notably the signing of the common programme in 1972 (Chevènement was the main PS negotiator for the economic chapters) and the insertion in it by Marc Wolf of a CERES priority, i.e. the famous clause whereby firms could be nationalised with parliamentary approval on the request of their workforce.

The fortunes of the French Left since 1972 have already

been described (see above); but so far as CERES goes, it may well seem in retrospect that the signing of the common programme represented to some extent the peak of its influence inside the PS. Increasingly, as some of the consequences of the unitary strategy became clearer, Mitterrand found it easier to rule with the support of more cautious elements inside the PS than with CERES, whose intransigence might well seem off-putting to the Centrist, floating vote. In 1975 at the Pau Congress, Mitterrand felt strong enough to dispense with CERES support. Refusing a synthesis between the CERES motion and that of his own supporters, he forced the group into a minority position (i.e. though still represented on the *comité directeur* and the *bureau exécutif* it lost its seats on the secretariat).

CERES remained in the minority after the Nantes congress of 1977 and was increasingly critical of the majority line during the failed re-negotiations of the common programme and the campaign for the 1978 elections. The defeat of the Left and the consequent recriminations within the Mitterrand-Rocard-Mauroy majority (or rather, the ex-majority) of the Socialist Party changed the perspective somewhat. As the Metz congress of April 1979 approached no less than seven motions were tabled — an eloquent testimony to the Party's fragmentation. For CERES the hope of another Epinay congress dawned; its votes might well be crucial to any majority that might emerge. In fact, Metz proved to be the way back into the secretariat and meant a revival of influence within the Party. The extent and nature of this will be discussed below; but it is now time to examine the essentials of CERES thinking and ascertain why the group has such a distinct profile inside the PS.

CERES THEORY

The characteristic arguments of CERES have changed little over the years, though the social and economic tensions generated by the crisis and the recriminations ensuing from the electoral defeat of 1978 have perhaps given them a sharper, more polemical edge than before. It is sometimes difficult to see exactly where a CERES stance on a particular issue begins to differ crucially from the views of either strands of the PS, for often the precise object of political discussion is lost under clouds of allusive polemic and personal attacks. This is so because these debates are taking place within a party that had not had so much as a toe-hold on office for over twenty years. There is thus no absolute means of knowing where the breaking points between CERES and the rest lie; this could only really be known if the party had withstood the acid test of governing. Thus until Spring 1981, all manner of speculation and innuendo as to the political consequences of the views of rival PS groups were legitimate. But bearing in mind these reservations, some characteristic preoccupations can be singled out.

(a) Analysis of contemporary capitalism

CERES sees the capitalist system as being in deep and enduring crisis, which it analyses in Leninist terms. Such analysis sees all parts of the world economy (except for the Communist bloc) as increasingly forming one unit, characterised by the dominance of the capitalist mode of production. Within this world economy is a dominant pole (the USA), where capitalism has developed furthest. This pole exercises hegemony over the other developed capitalist states and beneath them the Third World. Economic hegemony brings with it varying degrees of subordination in political, military and diplomatic relations. But the imperialist system (as Leninists describe the above) is today in crisis.

CERES and similar analysts see this crisis as stemming from an over-accumulation of capital. Since the mid-sixties the modern state has been unable to regulate, even with sophisticated interventionalist techniques, what is basically an over-accumulation of capital. The results of the crisis are well known — destruction of vast amounts of capital (bankrupticies, redundancies) increased concentration of capital (growth of the multinationals) and, most of all, a new international division of labour. This reorganisation of the world imperialist economy (CERES does not flinch from the term) is sponsored by its dominant pole, the USA, using both formal state power (e.g. monetary policy) and the power of private capital (principally the multi-nationals). Increasingly, older industries will be hived off to the peripheral countries; within Europe, increased economic integration and specialisation will become the rule. Only the most competitive will survive; hence governments will streamline their economies, encouraging only those few remaining industries with some potential and driving an increasing number of 'lame ducks' to the wall. The Barre plans were seen as the acceptance by the French state of this international situation.

These were a series of macro-economic measures which fit into the monetarist or deflationist tradition which has become all too familiar to British readers of late. Barre aimed to remedy a situation where the franc was losing value, the trade gap widening, inflation and unemployment rising, and investment stagnating. By putting discreet pressure on working people's incomes, Barre aimed to limit demand and reduce inflation (which he blamed on cost-push). Yet at the same time his encouragement of price rises allowed successful firms to increase profits considerably (Barre claimed that competition would keep price rises within reasonable bounds). Increased profits would, it was hoped, be ploughed back into investment, creating jobs and thus beginning a new upturn in the economy; after purgatory, paradise. These policies, then, are a vigorous rejection of Keynesian ones, which would seek to relaunch growth by stimulating demand above all. By 1981, despite some success with trade figures and the value of the franc, the plans had not stopped inflation from rising; in fact, what they did was to increase unemployment nearly to UK proportions, put many small businesses into bankruptcy and write off some of the older industries and declining regions of France. The higher profits did not reappear in the form of investment and there were no real signs of sustained expansion. How can socialists face up to this situation?

Unlike some of their colleagues, who tend to think that full-blooded socialism must be deferred in such an unfavourable climate, CERES argues the opposite. The crisis puts increased pressure on Western societies in fact; the working class, the intermediate white-collar strata or 'new petty bourgeoisie', the small farmer are all victims of the system's attempt to modernise itself, and they form the objective basis of a 'class front'. To them can be added as allies older strata (small businessmen, shopkeepers, etc.) also victims of the same process. The demands of such categories cannot by satisfied, says CERES, in any conventional democratic framework: because today, democratic demands necessarily become Socialist ones. CERES is specially critical of European social democracy, which it sees as having used office in an attempt to tide capitalism over its present difficulties; and in so doing it has positively retarded the chances of socialism in Europe. This view accounts for the crucial distinction that CERES makes between Socialism and Social Democracy and for the group's particular hostility to the Germany SPD and Portuguese Socialist Party.[4] In the emotive and allusive vocabulary in which CERES specialises, 'Bad Godesberg' and 'the Soares line' are, as it were, four-letter words. Clearly, much CERES polemic is aimed at would be or alleged immitators of North European Social Democracy inside the PS, and of late Michel Rocard whom CERES has long mistrusted, ever since he began to make a national reputation in the late 1960s, while still outside the Socialist Party, has been particularly singled out.

(b) Socialism and the transition from Capitalism

Like the rest of the Party (at least in theory) CERES calls for a self-managing socialism *(autogestion),* which is seen as being different from social democracy or state capitalism (this is how CERES would describe the régimes in Eastern Europe). Such an ideology involves the devolution of decision-making power as far as possible towards the grass-roots in every context — economic, political, cultural. Politically, this supposes a high degree of decentralisation of the French Jacobin state and, within the economy, the establishment of a far-reaching type of workers' control. Clearly to attain such a goal it is necessary to have an irreversible break *(la rupture)* with the logic of capitalism. For CERES the role of the state in such a break is crucial. The 1972 common programme pinned much of its economic strategy on nationalising key sectors of the economy, so as to ensure a basis for national planning. CERES was very attached to this strategy, as the public sector would not only assure a minimum of independence from the constraints of the world economy but also serve as a pilot area, where new forms of workers' control might be introduced. In this way, *la rupture* might be speeded up.

There is in all this an implied contradiction between the role of the state (as planner and economic 'motor') and the potential demands of self-managing workers in their workplace — even given the existence of a very supple type of democratic planning (for which neither CERES nor anyone else has a blueprint). But CERES insists that there can be no real progress towards workers' control or *autogestion* in the wider sense, unless the Left takes power and uses this power to possess the commanding heights of the capitalist economy. Other Socialists, especially Rocard, are mistrustful of the large shadow which the French state already casts over civil society[5]: indeed for Rocard, civil society has been virtually strangled by the state and needs resuscitation. Hence his sympathy for various types of 'social experiment' already taking place under capitalism: by this he means any kind of voluntary or associative activity (co-operatives, work-ins, etc.) which seems to offer a possibility of popular, anti-capitalist forms of organisation. Hence also Rocard's coolness towards nationalisation and what he sees as over-reliance on the state and a consequent faith in the market as regulator; hence also his warnings that the common programme would not automatically bring in *la rupture* (there would not be one *rupture*, but several spread over an indefinite period). CERES is bitterly critical of what it sees as an apolitical under-estimation of the importance of state power in the transition to socialism, and indeed a nostalgia for market liberalism. Rocard is thus presented as a virtual renegade who has turned his back on any break with capitalism; his commitment to *autogestion* appears hypocritical.

Another element of the transition is the constraint arising from France's insertion into the global economy. Many strands of the PS seem to accept that increasing French economic integration into Europe is inevitable. As Rocard's motion to the Metz congress has it[6]:

The businessmen's Europe has made its members so inter-dependent that there is no other solution for a Left government in France than to help in the building of a working people's Europe, i.e. *the creation of a coherent political and economic will* . . . the necessary line of resistance to American imperialism is to be found today at continental level (italics added).

CERES has always refused such logic, notably in its

campaign against the European Monetary System, which it saw as 'locking in' the French economy to that of West Germany with, as the most likely consequences, a low growth rate, austerity policies and the acceptance of a distinctly second rank as an industrial power[7]. CERES opposes further integration: it talks of re-negotiating the Rome treaty to preserve national sovereignty and stresses the need to 'recapture the home market' (presumably by protectionism) so as to reduce external dependence. Only thus can ailing sectors be revived, jobs created and a political alliance forged with the declining sectors of French capital who suffer from the opening outwards of the French economy.

To the charge that protectionism invites retaliation, CERES retorts that a protectionist cycle is probably on the way in any case and that one may as well as choose one's moment and strike first. As usual, it is argued that any socialist who shows indulgence towards the EEC or who makes more than a passing reference to the external constraints upon the French economy is an objective, if not subjective ally of Giscardian liberalism.

(c) The Party

If CERES' vision of the type of socialism it wants is uncompromising, then so too is its idea of the instrument for realising that goal, the Socialist Party. If the previous two areas of debate have seemed rather abstract, then this one is certainly not; it is perhaps the one where the clash between CERES and the rest is most bitter. What does the group understand by its phrase 'a party of transition and rupture'? Perhaps the question is best answered negatively. CERES does not want the new Socialist Party to be SFIO writ large, i.e. a party of voters based on a structure of well-entrenched local bosses with networks of clients. Equally, CERES refuses the democratic centralism of the Communist Party; for it, a genuine Socialist Party should be 'an organisation based on class-struggle, exempt from both the reformist and bolshevik deviations'[8]. The PS should be an activist, campaigning party.

One of the group's major reproaches to the Mitterrandist leadership was that between 1975 and 1979 it had taken the Party in the opposite direction, thinking in terms of a flabby, catch-all party[9]:

the chance of winning office has weighed too heavily on the minds of some
people for them to see what is really at stake in the building of 'a real Party,
a real Socialist Party'. Once they started preparing for power . . . the whole
party superstructure was turned into a sort of shadow cabinet, which was
more bothered about assuming responsibility at the head of state than
building an adult, autonomous party, working by itself and for itself'.

As well as the electoral concept of Party, CERES attacks
the more flexible idea associated with Rocard, whereby the
Party serves as a (rather indeterminate) link between groups
and associations in civil society, experimenting with various
types of self-management. Such an instrument is too weak to
withstand the challenge of using state power.

CERES wants the Socialist Party, then, to become a
campaigning Party, involved in all movements within French
society — industrial, regional, ecological, or whatever.
Unlike the rest of the Party it holds that electoral support will
be enhanced if it has such a bold profile. The privileged place
of action is seen as the workplace, and when CERES was on
the secretariat, Georges Sarre helped the number of
workplace groups to grow from 54 in 1971 to over 800 by late
1974. The Rightist Mitterrand-Mauroy axis was clearly
disturbed at this onset of activism, and one of the main
reasons for the eviction of CERES at Pau in 1975 was
Mitterrands's insistence that come what may the group
should relinquish control of the secretarial post dealing with
workplace branches.

The necessity for a strong PS presence in the workplace is
coloured by CERES expectations of what would happen in
the event of a Left victory at the polls and implementation of
the common programme. Numerous popular movements, as
in 1936 and 1968, were expected to flourish, catalysed
precisely by the Left's victory. These struggles would all be
aiming for control, but in different ways and at different
levels. But if they were not to peter out or become side-
tracked into economism[10] or worse, it was vital that a
structured force be there to link somehow these movements
to the work of government and help the government to
accelerate the rate of social change. The PS should be just
such a power.

Organisationally, CERES joins other currents (including

Rocard for once) in criticising the 'monarchical' way in which Mitterrand runs the top bodies of the Party. It wants more control of national office holders by members (notably the idea that the former should turn over their earnings to the Party, as in the Communist Party, and be paid a wage in return). CERES also wants more numerous and smaller branches, which it sees as more efficient as well as more democratic. It wants more autonomy for the youth and student movements of the Socialist Party, and it campaigns for the officialisation of tendencies inside the Party — a requirement that might seem superfluous in view of what has been said above.

In short CERES favours a more tightly structured and aggressive Party. Mitterrand accused it of wanting to make the Party into a 'fake Communist Party, made up of real petty-bourgeois'. But although there are superficial similarities between CERES and the PCF about Party organisation, although the group uses Leninist vocabulary (probably less nowadays), and although it is clearly fascinated by the cohesion and commitment of the PCF, there are nonetheless crucial differences with that organisation. These become apparent when we see the CERES view on Left union.

(d) Alliance Strategy and Union of the Left

It is important to counter the view that CERES is 'soft on Communism' or that it is some kind of Trojan horse whereby the PCF might somehow penetrate the Socialist Party. CERES in fact accepts a number of analyses of the PCF that are current within and outside the Socialist Party. Firstly, CERES says, as the PCF slowly de-Stalinises, it experiences an identity crisis, i.e. it is not sure what sort of party it will become. Secondly, it lacks any kind of project for French society that may help give it such an identity. CERES also accepts that PCF fears about being overtaken electorally by the Socialists and used as a 'hostage' in a future government were largely responsible for the PCF's breaking the unitary dynamic and losing the elections of 1978 for the Left. Finally, CERES has always held that unless it changes considerably the PCF will decline slowly from its 20 per cent or so of support, even though this decline may be a prolonged process: such an assumption was indeed central to the group's initial gamble in 1964.

But CERES adds to the above a number of riders, all of them relevant to the Socialist Party and its role in the alliance. Firstly the PS was also to blame for the Left's earlier defeat. Especially since the Nantes congress of 1977 its leaders behaved in a 'Gaullist' way, suggesting that theirs would be the major share in government, with the PCF very much a junior partner; in particular they refused any 'compromise over power'. This term, extensively used by CERES, is never really explained: but presumably at the very least it means spelling out exactly who would occupy what post in government well before an election and giving public guarantees about implementing certain pieces of legislation by certain dates. Failure to make such a compromise fed PCF paranoia; but it could have been different.

We come here to the heart of CERES thinking about Party and alliance; for the two have always been inseparable for CERES members. Left union is seen as a dynamic, which increases the strength of both parties, but in so doing tends to change them. Within the Communist Party it is likely to give a boost to those anti-Stalinist elements who seriously want to come to power and try to change France. But the only way in which such elements can exert influence on the PCF line, is paradoxically, if the Socialist Party is stronger. Stronger not just electorally (that on its own is fatal, in fact) but also by its organisation and campaigning presence everywhere in civil society: here of course is the key to CERES obsession with workplace branches. A stronger Socialist Party could then, so the argument runs, browbeat the Communists into following its lead: it would be hegemonic inside the alliance. It is stupid and mendacious to pretend that the two parties are somehow equal and non-competitive. The truth must be spelled out: the Socialists can and must lead, the Communists can only follow and in so doing change.

In the short term thus CERES wants Socialists to be more present in areas of social struggle and to undertake common (and competitive) grass-roots action at the side of the PCF (thus turning an old Communist tactic on its head, in fact). In the longer run, it looks forward to a new, detailed common programme, with a proper 'compromise about power'.

Clearly this strategy is bold and ambitious and open to numerous criticisms. But it does at least have the merit of calling a spade a spade and it certainly allows no-one to claim that CERES is soft on Communism.

(e) Foreign Policy

This area again shows sharp differences between CERES and others. Like others on the Left CERES has always been sensitive to a certain nationalist tradition which runs deep in Franch political culture. Thus Chevènement and his friends admire de Gaulle's idea of a 'national independence' for France, while being fully aware that militarily, economically and politically the General never possessed the means of realising his ambition. At any rate, CERES takes national independence desperately seriously. The aspiration towards independence underpins all CERES thought on foreign and economic policy. In foreign policy it favoured the idea of a 'geographical compromise' (privileged economic and political relations between Southern Europe, where the Left had a chance of power, and progressive states around the Mediterranean) which might afford room for manoeuvre away from the constraints of the international economy. But the progressive slipping away of power in Portugal from leftish, military-dominated governments to the aggressive conservatism practised lately by Sa Carneiro: the ebb of the Communist tide in Italy, when the Party seemed poised for office five years ago: the failure of the Spanish Left, where the Socialists are the strongest element, to dislodge Conservative governments steadily consolidating in the aftermath of Francoism, have all dealt blows to this vision.

As regards the EEC, hostility to integration has already been discussed and one must also note the group's fierce opposition to enlargement (in contrast to nearly all the rest of the socialists).[11] Interestingly, on the question of relations with European parties, the group has made numerous thinly-veiled hints to all opponents of integration, with a view to forming a common front. Although not mentioned by name, the Labour Left is clearly one object of such appeals[12]:

it would be desirable to organise an anti-capitalist front, European in the first instance, with all those forces which, especially within social democratic parties, are beginning to see the threat lying in wait for their societies and the lack of any answers from their own party.

CERES attacks any idea that existing EEC institutions can be used to develop Socialist policies and was very scornful of the common document signed by the Socialist Parties of the nine for the elections to the European assembly in 1979.

The other major thrusts of CERES foreign policy are unflinching anti-Americanism, attachment to an independent French nuclear force and desire to withdraw ultimately from the Atlantic alliance. It can hardly be emphasised enough how far these positions set it apart from the majority of a party that has always tended to be, to a greater or lesser extent, atlanticist, integrationist and pacifist.

(f) Ideology

It might seem odd to devote space to CERES' views on ideology, even in the context of a polity where value systems are always more explicit and arguments that much more abstract than in Britain. But it will be plain from the above how important a place ideology has in the internal debates of the Socialist Party. CERES has always privileged ideological themes in its discourse, not surprisingly perhaps in a group whose leaders are intellectuals of high calibre. But CERES has always understood the necessity of becoming culturally hegemonic, i.e. of creating a widespread acceptance of certain basic principles and assumptions, as the foundations of a successful political leadership by the Left. If the ideological dimension of CERES publications has increased of late, this is also connected with the fact that the French Right is currently staging an ideological offensive on various levels, notably in the sphere of economic theory (the 'new economists') and in philosophy (the 'new philosophers'). CERES' response to this has been wholesale denunciation of people within and close to the Socialist Party, whom it describes as 'the American Left'.

This label implies that much of the Left's thinking has become affected — unconsciously or willingly — by theories and assumptions of the Right. It will come as no surprise to learn that the main Trojan horse of the 'American Left' within the Socialist Party is Rocard. The major themes of such ideology are: (1) rejection of Marxism, often to the advantage of irrationalist philosophies or anarchistic notions of the type 'all power, especially state power, is bad'; (2) refusal of the state as an agent of social change, which is henceforth left to 'social experiment'[13]; (4) rejection of the nation as a meaningful framework for political or economic action. Whilst Rocard could not be accused of irrationalism or anarchism, his position on the other issues could certainly be questioned. CERES attempts to explain the theories of the 'American Left' as the ideology of the new petty bourgeoisie produced by modern capitalism; it is a rather pathetic attempt by this class to give itself some consistency or political identity. It must be made to see on the contrary that its political future depends on an alliance with the working class, based on correct Socialist policies (i.e. those endorsed by CERES). In other words, the label 'American Left' is the latest in a series which CERES has manufactured so as to characterise its opponents: this one stresses the cultural/ideological dimension, but in so doing inevitably runs on to other differences between CERES and its rivals.

At this point we can sum up the essence of CERES theory. Although the group shares basic assumptions with most of the Socialist Party (notably the general goal of a self-managing socialism), it has a distinct and quite firm profile on a number of issues concerned with the attainment of this goal — the nature of the Party and its alliances, the transition, the nature of Socialist foreign and defence policy (especially in the context of Europe), the importance of ideological rigorousness. It is now time to see how CERES propagates its ideas, i.e. to examine its structures inside the Party.

THE STRUCTURES OF CERES

These have grown from haphazard beginnings to a fair degree of sophistication, combined with some flexibility. Originally, when CERES activity was mainly Parisian and small in scale, members met regularly in a sort of permanent direct democracy, with only a small standing committee to ensure continuity. Today there are groups in most of France, at local, departmental and regional levels, links with Paris being assured by correspondents (who will meet in Paris at two- or three-monthly intervals). At national level there is a coordinating committee of some 100 people meeting at six- or eight-week intervals, with continuity assured by a secretariat which meets weekly (usually on Tuesday evenings to prepare for the *bureau executif* the following day). Hostile critics like the ex-CERES activist G. Martinet (now close to Rocard) allege that the 'historic leaders' of the group exercise an oligarchic power of decision similar to that which they denounce in rival organisations.[14]

Membership seems to involve different levels of commitment, ranging from activists who will probably hold office in the Party at large to a wider circle of sympathisers, who will vote for CERES motions without being active in or making any financial contribution to the group. The most generous estimate of CERES strength would have been some 40,000 in a Party of 190,000 after the Pau congress of 1975. The Metz congress of 1979 revealed a sharp decline, though; with 14.4 per cent of the delegate vote in a Party of around 160,000 CERES spoke only for some 22,000. There seems little by way of a permanent apparatus, nor are there the funds for one: as CERES has no membership cards, no fees can be levied and members pay on a voluntary basis (obviously many do not). The group has premises of its own in Paris, but nowhere else.

Much effort goes into propaganda, especially the printed word. At national level there is the review *Repères* (previously known as *Frontière* and *Cahiers du CERES)* which appears about ten times a year and is an articulate theoretical journal. It averages a sale of 20,000 copies. Since Easter 1980 it has changed its name to *Non!* and enlarged its list of contributors to include non-CERES writers. Perhaps this will give the review a boost which some feel that it has needed of late, given that some of its ablest writers have now gone to other currents. There is a shorter broadsheet *Volonté socialiste,* circulating mainly in Paris.

The other major national activity is a series of yearly or twice-yearly colloquia (weekend seminars), prepared by meetings at local and departmental levels and each taking a particular theme. This is where CERES as a whole thrashes out general policy outlines, which form the basis of motions presented to the Party nationally.

The impression emerges, then, of a structure which is

distinct enough to allow action by like-minded people but not particularly monolithic or centralised. Certainly CERES is better organised than either its predecessors in SFIO (e.g. the Pivert tendency of the 1930s) or other minorities inside European Socialist Parties.

CERES strength on national committees of the Socialist Party can be gauged more easily. The mechanisms of PR give it 21 seats out of 132 on the *comité directeur* and 4 out of 27 on the *bureau exécutif*. Within the Party secretariat CERES held 3 full posts and 1 junior one. Before 1981, only 6 deputies out of 103 were recognisably loyal to CERES, as were 3 senators out of 62: but this changed after the June elections (v. below). Some of the key leaders of the group sit on the secretariat — Motchane, Charzat, Guidoni.

In geographical terms, CERES is strongest where it began, viz. Paris, though it now has to share control of the Paris federation with the Mitterrandists. Its other heartlands are in the East, especially Belfort (where Chevènement is deputy), though lately it has progressed in industrial regions like the Loire department. Historically the East has not been good territory for the Left, tending to be nationalist and catholic; the fact that CERES has done well there (like the Party as a whole of late) says something about CERES activists.

CERES does not produce computerised breakdowns of sympathizers, any more than does the Party itself. But some evidence is available. According to a sample taken at a colloquium in 1974, the identikit picture of the CERES activist was of someone young, male, without previous political experience, white-collar with a high chance of being a teacher and slightly more likely than the average to be a practising Catholic.

A *Repères* survey of readers (who admittedly do not coincide exactly with CERES members, but who might well constitute the hard core of these) showed an even higher density of what might be called, in the wider sense, intellectuals[15]: public employees 40 per cent (of which 26 per cent teachers), students 24 per cent, other white collars *(employés)* 12 per cent, professions 6 per cent, upper management 2 per cent, farmers 2 per cent, workers 3 per cent.

Thus even allowing for the rule-of-thumb nature of these

samples, there seems little denying the intellectual character of CERES. This is probably true, to a greater or lesser extent, of other fractions in the Party, however. And it does not mean that the group's analysis of the French political situation, nor the strategy it recommends are necessarily vitiated by the class-origins of its members.

CONCLUSION: THE CERES ACHIEVEMENT THUS FAR, AND THE FUTURE

The turbulent approach to the Party congress of Metz in April 1979 and its triumphant outcome for CERES are recounted elsewhere in the volume. Despite a sharp drop in its delegate vote, CERES concluded an alliance with the Mitterrandists and regained places on the secretariat, forcing the Mauroy and Rocard supporters into opposition within the Party.

By mid-1980 CERES had been back in the Socialist leadership for a year, and it was possible to formulate some provisional conclusions about the group's situation and prospects. 1979-80 was not a good time generally for the Party, with membership beginning to level off, indeed decline, and an increasing irritability showing between the different currents, as the fight for the Socialist presidential nomination began in earnest between Mitterrand and Rocard. CERES tactics during this period continued the logic of the alliance that they had made at Metz: in other words they stuck as close to Mitterrand as possible, in the hope of stopping Rocard. It is in this context that one should understand the group's major effort of late, i.e. obtaining Party approval (in the special convention of January 1980) for the *Projet socialiste*. This was not a programme for the next elections, with the short-term analyses and figures that such documents entail, but a general statement of intent for the mid- and long-term. It does not thus supersede documents like the 1972 programme *Changer la Vie* or the 1975 theses on *autogestion,* but is seen as somehow deepening these. As such it is a very ideological document and bears signs (even in the amended version eventually accepted) of CERES authorship. This is particularly evident in the heavy stress on national independence and in the lengthy, erudite and frequently quite unreadable cultural and ideological analyses in which the text indulges. It also emerges in the subtle way in which the ideas of rival socialists such as Rocard (never named, in fact) are alleged to be merely re-workings of some of the oldest and tiredest ideas of the French Right: CERES reveals once more its talent for suggesting guilt by association. Clearly the document was intended for use by all sections of the current leadership as a rod for Rocard's back, should he ever succeed in becoming the Party's presidential candidate against their wishes. Certainly Rocardians have been in no doubt about this, criticising the *projet,* predictably, for state-worship and neo-Gaullist nationalism.

Through 1979-81 CERES was in fact paralysed by the imminence of the presidential elections, just like most of the rest of the Party. The group's worries increased as the possibility emerged that Mitterrand might not after all be a candidate: and Chevènement said that if this happened he would contest Rocard for the Party nomination. There is more at stake here than questions of personality, ideology or even policy. Victory by Rocard or even a narrow defeat in the second ballot in 1981 would have given him a legitimacy inside the Party possessed hitherto only by Mitterrand, who would presumably have retired in that event anyway. The next congress would surely have confirmed Rocard's authority, with most of the Mitterrand current probably swinging behind the new leader. CERES would be in a very exposed position: either it would be marginalised to the extent where many activists might feel ready to quit the Party, or else it would face long years of internal opposition until the Rocard bubble burst — in other words, the group would be put back ten years or more. Moreover the group might now have to face severe disciplinary sanctions from a Mauroy-Rocard majority determined to rid the Party of its Leftist image, which they see as deterring 'moderate' voters: compared to such an offensive, the previous administrative pinpricks sufferred by CERES might seem slight indeed. Alternatively, if Mitterrand were presidential candidate or even if he stayed on long enough to strengthen the ideology and organisation of his own current, he might be ready to carry on the alliance with CERES for a while yet, hoping that the Rocard current might fade as its leader's chance of national office receded. CERES could hope to use this respite to try and regain the 10 per cent or so of support that it has lost in the late seventies.

In the event history solved some of CERES' problems. Their own pressure, plus that of Mitterrand's allies, eventually forced the latter into standing for the presidency. The electorate's disenchantment with Giscard's economic and political record, plus the 'premeditated treason' of J. Chirac, did the rest, and the victory of May 1981 came as something of a 'divine surprise' to anyone who had seen the PS from close up six months before.

This victory was not, of course, as CERES had envisaged, i.e. a triumphant alliance of Communists and Socialists in which each Party transformed the other into an open, creative force for change, able to provoke mass movements in street and workplace. The Left union having run out of steam, the PCF was able to wage a morose and sectarian campaign against the PS, whose leader took a fairly prudent line, offering a package of demand-led reflation, albeit bolstered by a number of key nationalisations. But it would be hard to say that these amounted to a *rupture* as CERES has understood it. Moreover, Mitterrand's media campaign made much use of the 'American Left' in the shape of Rocard, whose reassuring virtues the PS leader appreciated only too well. By these means, then, Mitterrand managed what a French Socialist has to do if he is to win the presidency, viz. pull in enough floating voters from the centre, while at the same time reaching over the heads of the PCF leadership and 'filching' most of its voters without offering concessions (programmatic or otherwise). Mitterrand's win, and the party's amplified victory in June, were classic electoral triumphs, with the only mass movement being towards the polls. Clearly the voters wanted plausible change, not a sudden distortion.

Mitterrand's governments reflected this situation by rewarding the PCF with four technical posts and distributing most of the others among the PS tendencies, in a way that compels admiration. If Rocard was given a narrow brief at Regional Planning, the CERES was not exactly placed at the summit of the state apparatus. Chevènement's Research and Technology ministry threatened to be something of a white elephant, and if the new CERES recruit Nicole Questiaux got the important Social Security post, then the other CERES posts (E. Avice at Sports and F. Autain at Immigration) were minor. Economic policy was in the hands of P. Dreyfus at Industry (a former head of Renault) and J. Delors at Finance — a man whom CERES had tried to stop from joining the Party in 1974! Clearly there would be change, but very much at the rhythm which Mitterrand thought fit. Moreover there would be no witch-hunts against the losers of the Metz congress, for obviously Mitterrand intended to keep alive in government the quite impressive solidarity which the different tendencies had shown him during the campaign. CERES, then, had made some gains (not the least of which was the vast increase in its number of deputies from 7 to 36), but it now had to change from being a principled opposition to part of a government team. Although it is clearly too early to say how it has faced this task, there are some indications.

Despite the fact that the PS victory did not come about as they hoped and that the government is perhaps less radical than they would prefer, CERES seems to be taking a stance of fairly loyal support. Power, or a share thereof, is deemed more important than ideological purity. Thus although Chevènement fired some senior officials of the research councils (perfectly constitutionally, be it said) to replace them with men committed to change and although the October issue of *Non!* carried a slashing attack on what it perceived as Mitterrand's Atlanticism, the article was promptly disavowed by CERES leaders. More significantly, when J. Delors called in early December for a 'pause' in the spate of reforms, the first minister to leap, unsolicited, to his defence was Chevènement.

CERES strategy seems then fairly clear. It will use its position in government to gain extra legitimacy in party and country, and also to win back some lost support (hopefully by means more honest than those used at the Valence congress of October 1981, where CERES joined with the other three main tendencies to strip the Rocardians of several percent of their representation, without any votes being taken at branch or other levels). The progress of the tendency is clearly seen as being linked to that of the government as a whole. And on the horizon lies the 1988 presidential election, where Chevènement doubtless hopes to figure, especially if he can present himself between times as a responsible senior figure, mellowed by office. Clearly it is hard to say if this scenario will be fulfilled, especially if the government gets 'blown off course' and is tempted to resort to austerity measures. One imagines here that the CERES grass roots will be less disposed to compromise than their leaders might be. But so far CERES seems to be adjusting to the role of governmental faction with less difficulty than might be thought.

We are now in a position to attempt a summary of what has been achieved by CERES. It will be recalled that the original CERES decision to work within SFIO was something of a gamble. Some 15 years later it is possible to assess the wisdom of that gamble and to conclude that it paid off.

CERES was instrumental in the creation of the modern Socialist Party and has helped give this rather unstable amalgam its most characteristic features. The whole Epinay strategy of Left union, based on a common programme and the commitment to self-managing socialism (however much this concept still needs definition) would not have happened without CERES action — or certainly not anything like so quickly as they did. Few can doubt the efficacity of such a line in terms of the electoral and membership growth that it brought the party, whatever the misfortunes between 1977 and 1981. It is true that CERES was in opposition, within the Party, for four years; but even here it can be argued that its pressure stopped the Party from drifting further towards vagueness and unprincipled compromise. A small testimony to CERES influence is the very type of language that the Socialist Party — all factions alike — uses: phrases such as *'the rupture'*, *'the Epinay party'* have become almost obligatory (even for those who do not believe in them). Perhaps this makes it just a little harder for some to gloss over certain problems connected with the transition to that socialism which is, after all, the goal of the whole Party.

These results have only been achieved, however, because of the high degree of internal organisation and cohesion that CERES possesses. It may be true as the journalist T. Pfister claims that 'there is a real little party developing inside the PS, organising its own congresses and debating its own motions'[17]. CERES has always denied the 'party-within-a-party' accusation with some vehemence. Observers can judge for themselves the validity of such claims, but without wishing to go into speculation about the degree of organisation and specificity beyond which a group inside a party suddenly becomes a party in its own right, surely some type of organised faction like CERES is a necessary (some would say healthy) outcome of any party which is not monolithic and which does allow dissent? If groups with a common vision not shared by the leadership are unable to organise so as to make their views into party policy, then their influence is never likely to extend further than pious protest at party congresses (where they will be outmanoeuvred) or, if ever the party is in power, the odd rebellion in a parliamentary division. Of late other groups in the Socialist Party seem to have understood this much, as witness the Rocardians' attempts to organise themselves nationally, with their own review *Faire,* or the Mitterrandists' attempts to prepare for the eventual retirement of their leader by their diligent and well-publicised promotion of a new élite group (Jospin, Quilès, etc.).

CERES has shown that in a democratic party it is possible by intellectual clarity, political and organisational skill and hard work for a group of like-minded people, starting without any power-base inside the party, to exercise real influence in terms of policy and to give a certain image of that party to the public. The group has also made sure that certain awkward questions continue to be asked, preventing the party from slipping into complacency. And it has done this from *within* the party. The price of this has been a turbulent and at times quite nasty atmosphere inside the party; and of course the Right and those parts of the media sympathetic to it have made much capital out of this. But the unpleasantness has been open, unlike in many parties (where it is just as great): and no-one within the party has been allowed to ignore the matters under debate. Most people would probably hold that unity in a party is desirable, and few would disagree that such unity is better when it stems from genuine diversity. In the long run the CERES achievement might be to have shown that unity will in the end be even greater when based on *organised* diversity. Perhaps there is a lesson here for other parties.

Footnotes

1. Chevènement, Jean-Pierre. *Le Vieux, la crise, le neuf.* Paris, Flammarion, 1975. p.11 ff.
2. By workerism is understood the belief that within socialist movements primacy should go to manual workers, as opposed to other social groups, e.g. intellectuals. The doctrine thus puts more emphasis on the class-origins and the cultural distinctness of socialists than on their capacity for political analysis. It has always a strongly anti-intellectual flavour, though this does not of course prevent it from being employed on occasions by intellectuals.
3. Charzat, Michel: Chevènement, J.P. and Toutain, G. *Le CERES — un combat pour le socialisme.* Paris, Calmann-Lévy, 1975. p.21.
4. Cf. *Repères* 55-6 (Jul.-Sep. 1978) p. 17, where a Social Democratic Party is defined as 'a mass Party, bringing together or attempting to bring together the greater part of the working class and middle classes so as to defend their interests with out challenging the structures of capitalism (private appropriation by capital, laws of the market, national and international division of labour)'.
5. 'Civil society', usually used in opposition to the 'state', is an old concept of political theory which has been revived in this century by Gramsci and numerous Left theorists since. Crudely speaking, the concept suggests that the citizen's life can be seen under two heads, public and private. On the one hand there is his formal political activity at local or national level, which is seen as relating to the state; on the other is his private life (economic activity, culture and ideology, involvement in voluntary groups) which he lives in civil society. Clearly this distinction was never particularly watertight and is becoming ever less so. See the debate in *Nouvelle Revue Socialiste* 37 (Jan. 1979) on 'social experiment' between representatives of all main PS currents, including Chevènement and Rocard, for further insight into this problem.
6. *Le Monde* 16 February 1979.
7. Sandeau, Jacques. 'Barême: pavane pour un boa constrictor' *Repères* 58 (Nov. 1978) pp.46-55.
8. Charzat *et al. op.cit.* p.197.
9. *Repères* 55-6. p.9.
10. Economism is a term used by Marxists to describe working class actions and strategies, especially in a trade union context, which pursue short-term economic gains (e.g. over pay or hours) at the expense of longer term political goals (the development of socialism). The latter goals are seen as demanding more political consciousness on the part of workers.
11. Cf. Guidoni's article in *Repères* 55-6 (pp.126-31) in which CERES acceptance of enlargement is made conditional upon terms which the group knows perfectly well to be politically unrealistic.
12. *Repères* 53-4. (May-Jun. 1978) p.83.
13. CERES is highly scornful of Rocard's theory that the French Left contains two political cultures, one statist and centralising, the other libertarian and experimental. This is seen as an alibi for avoiding the necessary rigour of nationalisation and planning.
14. Bizot, Jean-Pierre. *Au Parti des socialistes.* Paris, Grasset, 1975. p.235.
15. *Repères* 53-4, pp.63 ff.
16. *Le Monde* 31 October 1981.
17. *Le Monde* 17 December 1978.

PART THREE:
THE COMMUNIST PARTY

By D.S. Bell

CHAPTER ONE

The Evolution of French Communism

INTRODUCTION

Since 1958, the beginning of the Fifth Republic, the French
Communist Party has been the key to the situation on the
French Left. However the PCF is a difficult Party to
understand; closed, secretive, bureaucratic, Stalinist and
thoroughly difficult to deal with, it represents a major
problem to Socialist Party leaders who have to come to terms
with it and it is an object of considerable suspicion to the
French electorate — as opinion polls reveal.[1] But it is to the
French Communist Party that the observer must turn, to
explain the position of the contemporary French Left as it is
on that Party's behaviour that people must concentrate to
understand the movement out of the Fifth Republic impasse.
Events of the late 1970s will be treated below, as will the
relations between Communists and Socialists, but the
essential starting point for a study of the PCF is an overview
of its historical evolution.

PCF 1920-1958

The French Left ostensibly puts a high value on unity but as
noted above only for a short period has the French Labour
Movement been united in anything like the British, German,
or Scandinavian sense and that was the short period from the
creation of the SFIO in 1905 to 1920. In December 1920
occurred the major split between the Communist Party
adhering to the Bolshevik international and the mainstream
democratic socialist tradition represented by the SFIO under
Léon Blum and now the *Parti Socialiste*.

French Socialists at Tours disagreed over a number of
issues but prominent amongst them were the Communist
view of the revolutionary collapse of capitalism, internal
party organisation and discipline, the twenty-one conditions,

and Moscow control.[2] Tours saw the dispersal of French Socialist energies in internal Left disagreements, a situation from which it has never fully recovered. When the parties split the Communists took the majority of party activists and the SFIO kept most of the parliamentary party. Despite these considerable advantages, and the inheritance of the Socialist newspaper *L'Humanité,* the Communist Party's membership and votes fell through the 1920s.[3]

Declining Communist influence was due to a number of factors. There was the persistent internal warring of the Communists plus the fact that early Communists were a diverse group so that the imposition of Moscow control on them was difficult and costly. Furthermore the recovery of the SFIO was rapid and contrasted with the dogmatic and inappropriate Communism of the time. This feature of the PCF which was underscored by their campaign after 1928 on the line that the SFIO was the main enemy and which included the refusal to withdraw its candidates on the second ballot.

Communist fortunes were no better at the beginning of the 1930s when the party was isolated, intransigent, and beset by internal rivalries. The 1932 election left the PCF with only eight deputies and just over 700,000 votes and limited influence in the trade unions where it pursued the policy of division through the maintenance of a separate union structure. None of this was, however, much of an indication to future potential and the party had come under the control of Stalin's Maurice Thorez by the 1930s.

A real change on the French Left came with the implementation of the Popular Front strategy in mid-February 1934.[4] Until that time Communists had disrupted the Assembly and fought 'social fascism' (i.e. the SFIO) but on the change of line the PCF adopted the course of SFIO and Communist alliance championed until then by the Socialist Left. This abrupt change in line came as a result of the needs of Stalin's foreign policy, Communist claims to the contrary notwithstanding, but it proved a winner in almost every field.

In the 1936 'Popular Front' election the PCF made big gains to poll 1½ million votes and elect 70 deputies, though they gained most of these from Léon Blum's SFIO. Although the Communists refused office in the Popular Front government they got the best of both worlds because they were able at one and the same time to reap the prestige from the reforms and gain from obstructive opposition to the Blum Socialist government. A prospect of a government with Communist support, and perhaps participation, had been opened out and the PCF had adopted a parliamentary strategy.[5] However the Popular Front policies were Socialist, not Communist, and the Communist Party line was a tactical one to meet the exigencies of the day not a new long-term strategy for Socialism. It is doubtful, therefore, whether the Popular Front stands as a precedent for anything let alone 'Eurocommunism' or 'Left union' in the 1970s.

So much was demonstrated by the breakdown of the Popular Front amid mutual recriminations and with great bitterness. A complete U-turn in Communist Party policy was signalled by the Nazi-Soviet pact whereupon the Communist Party started to denounce British imperialism and the imperialist war. Had the government not reacted by banning the PCF, the Communists would probably have been in much greater difficulties. As it was the Communist Party was caught in the general demoralisation of the defeat by Hitler and subsequent administration. Some Communist leaders went into hiding (Thorez deserted his army unit to spend the war in Russia) but offered to testify against Léon Blum's 'crimes' for Petain's Vichy and they seem to have expected to be allowed to exist in legality under the occupation. This is a period of PCF history which the Party itself hardly mentions but which it has still to come to terms with, although the PCFs initial bewildered reaction does not appear to have been all that different from most Frenchpeople at the time.

After the German attack on Russia in May 1941 things changed. Thereafter the PCF threw itself into the Resistance with a will with the result that by 1944-45 it had come to be seen as the political party of patriotism and struggle against invaders.[6] As a consequence of the big role the Communists played in the war in occupied France the party gained in prestige and extended its following so that at the end of the war the Communists had penetrated many social milieux. Communist activity in the *maquis* guerrilla and their use of sympathisers gave them influence in areas hitherto closed to Communists such as some agricultural areas, the main trade unions, and so on.

In 1945, at the Liberation, the Communists with 26 per cent of the votes emerged as a dominant force in France, organised, disciplined and benefitting from the Resistance struggle, the prestige of the Red Army, and promising radical social reform. There are those who say that the PCF backed down from the open possibility to take power in France at this time. What they did do was to pay off many old scores not only against collaborators. However the possibility of a Communist insurrection was abruptly removed from the agenda when, as a result of a deal between de Gaulle and Stalin, Maurice Thorez the Party leader returned from Russia where he had spent the war. Thorez immediately called upon Communists to surrender the arms they had seized from the retreating Germans and started to purge the Party of those who had been too prominent in the Resistance and who therefore did not owe their position entirely to the leadership. Conversely Thorez began to promote people who had either no Resistance record or whose past was slightly murky i.e. those who owed their loyalty to Thorez and the Party alone. This is possibly when the present Communist Party leader, Georges Marchais, who war past is decidedly obscure, began to move up the Party bureaucracy.

Being a major force at the Liberation the Communists were made a part of the government by de Gaulle.[7] Amongst their Ministers were Maurice Thorez, François Billoux and Arthaud, but there were several tensions in this position. One was the constant pressure from the extreme Left at a time of rationing and inflation plus a deteriorating international situation so that the Communists were participating in governments engaged in fighting colonial wars in Vietnam and Madagascar. The 'tripartite' coalition of Communists, Socialists and Christian Democrats broke down in May 1947 when the Socialist Prime Minister used the occasion of a vote by Communist deputies against the government wages policy to dismiss the PCF Ministers.[8]

Communist Ministers therefore left the government on 5 May 1947 without, it must be said, the consequences being entirely obvious at the time. The post-war years saw the coming and going of governments with considerable frequency but this change was regarded as merely another re-shuffle. Yet events moved fast in the following months. First the Communist opposition to Marshall Aid and the beginning of the Cold War led to the steady polarisation of feeling in France into pro- and anti-Communist. In Autumn 1947 Communists in France and Italy orchestrated a series of popular strikes which started with some astonishing incidents in Marseilles and quickly spread, based, as they were, on radical discontent. In the fearful atmosphere of the late 1940s these were interpreted as a Communist attempt to seize power although this seems unlikely, and a more probable explanation is that they were an attempt to show that Communists were indispensable allies in any post-war government.[9]

In fact what the November strikes did was to drive the Communists into a ghetto and to form a crevasse between them and the non-Communist Left. This instituted the period of Third Force policies for the Socialists, that is of alliances of the centre and of reformists opposed both to conservatism and the PCF (in fact the SFIO later formed alliances with many conservative groups). Communist tactics also ushered in a period of fierce anti-Communism based on the fear of Communist infiltration, a fear which appeared to have been confirmed by the November 1947 strikes.

Communist Party-instigated strikes split the union movement into pro-CGT (the biggest part) and anti-Communist (the FO) and permanently weakened the union movement in France. But the strikes and mass demonstrations did not stop in 1947, they continued through the years to the anti-Ridgeway riots in 1953 after which they began to taper off. Internationally the French Communists adopted a position of unconditional support for the Soviet Union. All of these events served to emphasise Communist isolation and made a rapprochement with the Socialists impossible — not that they seemed to want one.

The French Communist Party survived Stalin's death and the Hungarian uprising with barely a second thought but they did play a more important role within the French system — possibly with a view to re-integration — during the period 1953-1958. Notable on this count were the Communist

opposition to the proposed European Defence Community
and the support for the Mollet (Socialist) government of
1956. Communists took a particularly ambiguous line on the
Algerian war, placing as their primary concern an alliance of
some sort with the Socialists, but although *L'Humanité* was
seized on several occasions the PCF did not play the most
eminent role in opposition to the war.[10]

During the Fourth Republic the decline of the Socialist
Party and the ghetto position of the PCF (which managed to
retain around 25 per cent of the vote) meant that there were
few pressures on it to de-Stalinise and, unlike the Italian
Party, it stood pat on its old certainties but without making
much of an impact. PCF demonstrations against the fall of
the Republic in 1958 carried little conviction and made no
impact on public opinion.

THE FIFTH REPUBLIC

Under the Fourth Republic the Communist Party had
survived in its isolation and had probably gained from the
discomfort of the SFIO and the lack of a credible non-
totalitarian Socialist Party. Its election results show in this
that it had obtained a persistent 25 per cent of the vote (26.2
per cent in 1945, 161 deputies) and in the last election of the
Fourth Republic it managed 25.9 per cent of the vote and 150
deputies which contrasted with the SFIO's 15 per cent and 99
deputies.[11]

Yet the arrival of de Gaulle on the scene in 1958 made
major inroads into the Communist vote. It is important to
remember that de Gaulle had a genuine popular support and
in 1958 polled amongst the working class and Communists as
no other figure or Party since the rise of the PCF in 1936.
Thus at the referendum on the constitution in 1958 many
Communists ignored their leaders' advice to endorse de
Gaulle, in the October 1958 elections the Communist vote
slumped to 19 per cent (a 6.5 per cent drop) and under the
new electoral system of two ballots the voters used the second
round to combine against the PCF to reduce its Assembly
representation to a mere 10.

Communist difficulties were caused by de Gaulle's position
as a national leader of heroic status and, in particular, by his
status as the man who could end the Algerian war — *la salle*

guerre. Nevertheless the Communists could hardly allow this situation to go unchallenged and the PCF began to do some re-thinking so that by 1962 (the next legislative elections) the Party was willing to do a deal with the SFIO to save seats in the Assembly. What is more important is that Maurice Thorez, still the PCF leader, introduced the policy of Left union, that is the creation of a Socialist, Communist, Radical alliance echoing the Popular Front which would have a common programme of measures agreed for a specific governmental period.[12] A common programme was seen as essential because of the believed Socialist tendency to renege on commitments; but the policy was a long haul policy and the mutual suspicion on the Left was such that it could hardly have been implemented immediately. First steps in this direction were taken in secret Communist/Socialist meetings and in the informal agreement to support the leading Left candidate on the second ballot in November 1962.

Communists took a patient attitude of waiting for the SFIO to move towards the PCF, rather than one of forcing the pace of things. Maurice Thorez died in 1964 and was replaced by Waldeck-Rochet at the head of the Party. In retrospect Waldeck-Rochet may appear as the 'John 23rd' of the PCF for, although he continued Thorez' strategy of Left union, he began to liberalise the Party in his slow manner. Waldeck-Rochet began to modernise Communist doctrine to come to terms with the rise in living standards in the West and de-Stalinisation in the Soviet Union, though these changes were hesitant.

Waldeck-Rochet's new leadership coincided with the beginning of the 1965 presidential election campaign. De Gaulle was an obvious winner and had the PCF put up a candidate, they would probably have lost votes to him, at any rate they could not be sure of their own showing. This factor plus the Communist keenness on a united Left approach led them to support François Mitterrand as the Left's candidate from the first ballot. Before arriving at the endorsement of Mitterrand as the Left's common candidate along with the SFIO there were numerous difficulties which the Party had to negotiate notably the attempt by Defferre to float a Centre/Left presidential candidate to freeze out the Communists. Defferre's attempt failed through internal disagreements and the field was left open to Mitterrand who nevertheless kept the PCF at arm's length notably by keeping his actual programme vague.

Mitterrand's success in forcing de Gaulle to a run-off, collecting 45.5 per cent of the vote, encouraged the Left generally and gave heart to the Communist campaign for Left union. Tentative steps were taken by the Party towards liberal positions with the publication by *l'Humanité* in 1966 of some criticisms of the USSR. These slight openings to the outside ran parallel with consolidation on the non-Communist Left and the 1967 elections improved the coherence of the Left with the Communists managing 22.5 per cent of the vote (73 seats) and the FGDS (Radicals, Mitterrand supporters and SFIO) getting 19 per cent — 116 seats. But the events of 1968 were to prove a considerable setback to this developing Left union.

Communist attitudes to the student unrest at the beginning of 1968 are well known and their attitude to 'petty bourgeois' students was cool as Marchais made clear at the time. An effervescent quasi-anarchist/*gauchiste* spontaneous student movement was the last thing that the Stalinist bureacracy of the PCF could be expected to understand and the May 'events' burst on a Communist Party as ill-prepared as the rest of France. However the PCF having chosen the parliamentary strategy did not intend to be pushed into revolution at the behest of a student movement against its own judgement. Communists in the factories, the CGT, and ordinary activists worked to draw off the anti-system impact of May eventually re-gaining control of the strikes that had outrun their own activists.[13]

In June 1968 the elections put an end to the insurrectionary atmosphere but the PCF saw its vote go down to 20 per cent its deputies to 34 and the non-Communist Left was reduced to 16.5 per cent (57 deputies). What was worse for the PCF was that the May events destroyed the steady progress towards Left union (the Left had gone as far as to produce a common platform in 1968) and broke up the non-Communist Left's congealing unity. Communists did not lose entirely from May 1968 for a large number of activists seem to have moved into the PCF after May as the Party represented the only organised Left of any size at that time.

But 1968 produced a further shock for the PCF: the Russian invasion of Czechoslovakia. Prior to its occurrence French Communists do not seem to have regarded the possibility of an invasion as likely but once the invasion had taken place they condemned Russian actions. Waldeck-Rochet thus kept faith with his to some extent moderate liberalising, thrust but the pressures from Moscow and within the Party were intense with the result that the initial disclaimer was subsequently qualified to the extent that they began to approve the Czech 'normalisation'. Fierce battles raged within the French Party which still included a large pro-Soviet group. Waldeck-Rochet became 'ill' so that from 1968 until 1972 when Georges Marchais was made General Secretary the Party went through a confused, troubled period which saw the expulsion of Garaudy (the Marxist-Christian) in a seeming hardening of attitudes.[14] This hardening was perhaps shown in the PCF's running of the old Stalinist Duclos in the 1969 elections. Duclos got a good 21.5 per cent vote but there was   no real Socialist challenge and, underlining their refusal to vote for Centrists, they called on their supporters to boycott the second ballot.

In fact the election of Marchais as Communist leader was thought to be largely the Moscow influence because he was preferred to Roland Leroy who in 1968 had been in Prague and profoundly marked, so it is said, by the invasion. Be this as it may, Marchais continued the Thorez-Waldeck-Rochet strategy of moving towards Left union on a common programme and Marchais also stood by the 1968 'Champigny Manifesto' which (even in December 1968) made no concessions to revolution and mapped out a parliamentary road to socialism in a liberal direction.

In this context the PCF brought out its own programme *Charger de Cap* in 1971 as a negotiating position for discussions over a Common Programme with the New Socialist Party. In June 1972 a common programme was signed with the Socialists, an event which the Party regarded as their real triumph and they probably expected to gain from this pact in much the same way as they gained from the Popular Front.[15] But, despite throwing their own activists massively into the promotion of the Common Programme the Socialist Party was the principle beneficiary.

The 1973 legislative election did not presage great changes on the Left. The Communist Party maintained its position as the dominant force on the Left with 21.3 per cent of the vote (73 deputies) although the union of the non-Communist Left climbed up to 20.8 per cent (101 deputies). There was nothing to perturb the quiet progress of the Left from which all Left Parties were able, so it appeared, to gain. Communists, relying on the strength of their organisation to regain positions lost after 1968, made some of the running in demonstrations in late 1973 but the climate on the Left was good and neither inflation nor austerity had yet begun to bite.

This was the position when president Pompidou unexpectedly died in May 1974. Mitterrand was the obvious Left candidate and the Communists saw no reason not to back a single candidate from the first ballot. They therefore endorsed Mitterrand and put their formidable machine at his disposal. Mitterrand's campaign was very much an individual one, he made few enough references to the common programme, and the PCF's contribution to Mitterrand's near success was to be as amenable, quiet, and accommodating as possible. This is the high point of Left union for Mitterrand's campaign united the the entire Left to the extent that it was a matter of a mere 400,000 votes in 26 million between Giscard and the Left.

Communist orators congratulated Mitterrand on his campaign but something happened in the summer of 1974 within the Party for in the autumn by-elections showed that the Socialists were gaining disproportionately and the party leashed attacks on the *Parti Socialiste* which have been going on ever since. These attacks probably have their origin in internal Party disputes because those who distrusted the Socialists grouped, as far as can be gathered, around Roland Leroy, gained the upper hand, took Marchais by surprise and forced a hardening of Party line at the PCF's 1974 Vitry-sur-Seine congress. Marchais fought back and seems to have regained control of the Party so that the liberalisation of the PCF continued throughout the mid-1970s though without completely stopping the anti-Socialist polemic.

The 22nd Party Congress is probably the high point of Communist opening out.[16] This was the congress which unveiled 'Socialism in French colours' and where Marchais announced the abandonment of the dictatorship of the proletariat doctrine. One thing that was not touched was the party organisation which remained intact and made possible an abrupt reversal of line at anytime — as indeed happened. Other events seemed to confirm the liberalisation, for example, the 'operation open heart' which allowed visitors to enter the party's enormous head office, watch cell meetings etc (the Paris Federation was particularly prominent in this process).

All the PCF's liberalism was tempered by counter-currents. If the Party condemned Russian violations of human rights and published a manifesto of 'liberties' it also supported the Portuguese Communist suppression of the Socialist journal *Republica* in Portugal. If the Party was marking its distance from Moscow it retained its formidable, disciplined apparatus intact. Moreover the liberation was a necessary part of the strategy of Left union and that strategy could be changed at short notice.[17]

Municipal elections in March 1977 were good for the Left and the Communist Party, hitherto vigorously excluded from local government, moved into association with the Socialists at local level and as a result gained enormously. Yet the basis for Left unity, the Common Programme, had been negotiated in 1972 and five years later it needed to be updated. The balance of forces on the Left had changed considerably since the original negotiation and Socialist views had changed. Communists published a costed account sheet of the Common Programme on the eve of a TV debate between Mitterrand and Prime Minister Raymond Barre which did nothing to help the Socialists. This was the escalation of a smouldering dispute which ultimately caused the breakdown of the Left union in the autumn of 1977 just a few months before the legislative elections of March 1978 which all the polls indicated that the Left could, and should, have won.

The causes of the breakdown are discussed below but for the Communists it was the signal for the polemic against the Socialists to take off into a new level of intensity. As a result of persistent Communist attacks on the Socialist Party the Left lost the 1978 legislative elections and Communists retained a hold on their electorate which they had feared that they were losing. These elections gave the Communist Party 20.56 per cent of the vote but they were passed for the first time since 1936 by the Socialist Party which won 22.59 per cent of the vote (the Left Radicals got 2.11 per cent).

Subsequent to the 1978 election the Communists were much more concerned to reinforce the position of their own Party than to seek out common ground on the Left. They ran a very strong anti-European Community campaign in 1979 (in rural areas especially) and probed Socialist weaknesses wherever possible. These seem to have taken place in the perspective of Marchais as Communist candidate for the 1981 presidential elections but there was also a distinct hardening of line and a turning towards Moscow — these are also discussed below.

The 1970s therefore show contradictory features in French Communism and provide features which can be built on in the 1980s though in quite what way will be difficult to say. These are themes which will be taken up next.

THE FRENCH COMMUNIST PARTY 1978-1982

French Communists had been calling for Left union 'at the summit', that is between the main Parties of the Left in a new Popular Front, since Thorez' days and the first mention of a common programme is probably Thorez in 1962. Communists in France apparently imagined that Left union would benefit them in much the same way as it did in the mid-1930s when the Popular Front gave it a breakthrough and made it a massive national Party. Unlike the Italian or Spanish Communists the French Party saw no reason to de-Stalinise and the weak non-Communist Left gave then no competition. French Communists therefore called for an alliance with the Socialists aware that they needed Socialist support but believing that they would be the main beneficiaries from such an alliance and unaware of the need to cut their links with the Stalinist past.

The PCF under Thorez, then Waldeck-Rochet and then Marchais made considerable sacrifices to bring about Left unity and although there were persistent grumblings from the Communists the position was amicable enough on the Left even though the Socialist Party was growing rapidly whilst the PCF was not. All this changed with the by-elections of September 1974 which provided the impulse to a Communist change of line when they revealed spectacular Socialist growth and Communist stagnation (possibly even some losses). From that date in 1974 to 1978 the history of the French Left is the story of a long series of Communist attacks on a growing Socialist Party. These attacks probably had the objects of weakening the Socialist Party if need be at the expense of a Left victory at the polls and of rebuilding the Communist Party as the dominant Party of the French Left. It is a time of Communist mass recruitment (building membership up to a putative 700,000) and of liberalisation (baptised 'Eurocommunism').

If the Communist Party hoped to redress the balance on the Left by building itself up and by refraining from a too-blatant destruction of Socialist credibility things changed in the 1978 elections. At these elections the PCF opened out its attacks to preserve its position at all costs: this strategy paid off because it polled over 20 per cent, a respectable figure even if the PS had 22.5 per cent. However 1978 marks the end to Left union and the beginning of the PCF's inward march.

French Socialists, of course, remained open to the rebuilding of Left union which had served them well but there were no favourable signs from the PCF. The French Communist Party one by one began to reject or drop the policies which it had adhered to during the high days of Left union. Criticism of the PCF's behaviour during the 1978 elections came from such isolated intellectuals as Elleinstein and Althusser and discontent seemed to be strong inside the Party and the CGT unions but these individuals were easily dealt with by the leadership using the Party machine to crush them. It is difficult to be sure how much damage the change of line did to the Party: it is clear that it opened out dissidence which overflowed into the 'bourgeois' press and it lost activists but they were probably expendable as far as the Party was concerned.

As the PCF started to prepare for its 23rd Congress dissent inside the Party seemed to be growing and in an attempt to draw off the worst aspects of this a meeting was called in December 1978 at Vitry for 'intellectuals'. But the academic lap-dogs who composed the Communist 'intellectuals' were not all appeased by this ostensibly 'liberal' gesture — of course no concessions were made. The 23rd Congress at Saint-Ouen in May 1979 was conducted along classic democratic centralist lines. An indication that the Party was getting increasingly intemperate was the decision to start throwing leading dissidents off the sledge. The dissolution of the Paris Federation — where the Left union heresy was rooted — and so Henri Fizbin was 'resigned' from the head of the Federation and those too critical of the Party's hard line towards the Socialists were demoted.

In the event the leadership's texts for the 23rd Congress were decidedly illiberal. Turning their backs on the critical view of Russia which had been evolving in the Party the account sheet of the Eastern bloc was described as 'generally positive' (a phrase which has since become notorious). A quasi Cold War tone was introduced into the Party's international discourse and of course, the Socialist Party was placed along with other Social Democrats like Labour, in the imperialist camp.

French Communists had begun to speak about *autogestion* (self-management) as the rest of the Left had begun to drop it in 1978 but this term did not mean a new flexibility — it fitted into the old Communist algebra. *Autogestion* meant control by the PCF which was as rigid and centralised as ever and which, the leadership underscored, would not be relaxed. A pre-EuroCommunist Rip Van Winkle would have recognised many of these themes: a pro-Russian foreign policy, the emphasis on the capitalist crisis, condemnation of American war-mongering and the Social Democratic accomplices, and union of the Left 'from below' — i.e. no Left union at all.

In addition to the change of Communist line at the Congress the party leadership changed the composition of the Politburo and Secretariat. Marchais rivals inside the party were smashed down with Leroy and Piquet being removed from the Politburo. There were then promotions of the Marchais faithful notably Gremetz and Moreau so that Marchais had clear command over the party. The subsequent hardening of the party line and attacks on the Socialist Party cannot therefore be attributed to the forcing of Marchais' hand: they were the party's strategy to redress the balance with the Socialists.

French Communists after the 23rd Congress threw themselves into the battle for the European elections. The PCF turned to populist nationalism as a way of compensating for the loss of Left union as a mobilising issue and made a good deal of the running in rural areas on the deleterious effects of enlargement to Portugal, Greece and Spain but it also pointed out the challenge to French industry. The result, on a reduced poll, was a creditable 20.59 per cent (4,101,052 votes) and the party seemed, at that time, to have ridden out the storm over the disruption of the Left.

French Communists had not, however, made any impact on the Socialist Party. The vote for the PS at the European elections was bad in that they had expected more and (with the MRG) 23.73 per cent was down on 1978 but the PCF had not succeeded in pulling the PS over to the Left: Mitterrand remained inflexible and deaf to Communist appeals. But the Communist Party felt that it could use the rising discontent over unemployment and working conditions to increase its audience in the working class. Again this was not particularly successful and the workers' council elections showed that the Communist-run CGT was losing votes to the Socialist oriented CFDT. Nevertheless the CGT continued to try to capitalise on industrial issues running campaigns (like the blockade of northern ports) into the 1981 elections to demonstrate Communist implacability and determination on behalf of the worker — this was industrially and electorally counter-productive.

Communists were faced with a falling Party membership (as far as can be gathered from the dubious figures) and a demo-bilisation of their supporters generally. The reaction was to fling itself even more vigorously into the industrial front where, it calculated, its experience and organisation would count. Attacks on the government and on the Socialists went along with mass meetings on these problems. It became in-creasingly evident that, like everybody else, the Commu-nists had their eyes fixed on the 1981 presidential elections.

Within this framework the Communists ran a number of hares as well as the industrial disruption one. There were the racial campaigns of winter 1980 and the meetings with Communist leaders (to emphasise Marchais statesman-like qualities).

As noted (see above) the background in which the Communist Party presented its pillowy thesis of conceit and rancour was not appreciated by the electorate which gave Marchais a first ballot of 15 per cent. To some extent this was a censorship of the Party's numbskull populism but it was also, as the PCF underlined very heavily, the consequence of a an election system which must work against the PCF. However it is m ore than this because Communist voters turned out to support Mitterrand against their 'own' candidate in solid Communist areas. These things must be difficult for the party to swallow because the Socialists were undoubted victors but the party apparatus does not transmit such shocks directly to the leadership.

Although the legislative elections were scarcely better for the PCF it did win 16 per cent of the vote. But these elections saw the Communist Party cut down in many areas including Paris where it lost the seats of Mme Gisèle Moreau, Paul Laurent, and Lucien Villa to Socialists. Communist representation in the Assembly was cut by half to 44 and the electoral, sociological, and political relationship with the Socialists was completely overturned. Realising this the PCF abruptly changed tactics after the first round of the presidential election and began to demand its 'rightful' place in the new government which, went in hand with a Heapish praise for the Socialist victory.

The Socialist Party had no illusions about the loyalty of this support: it would disappear when the PCF felt it could draw some profit from criticising the government. During the 'honeymoon period' the PCF put itself solidly behind the government but it has placed on record various criticisms which it can take up later and has run campaigns which indirectly criticise the government such as that against the N-bomb and the massive anti-nuclear demonstration in Paris at the end of October 1981.

However the Socialists realised that they would need to ally with the Communists in the future and they wished to prolong the president's post-election 'honeymoon' (which Marchais had once stated would be one of strikes) and so the Communists were given four Ministries — the first since 1947.

The Communist Ministers were M. Charles Fiterman who

is Marchais' right-hand man and who had distinguished himself in the past by his attacks on Mitterrand, M. Anicet Le Pors, M.J. Ralite and M.M. Rigout. Fiterman was made Minister of State for Transport but the sensitive defence area of the Ministry was removed from him. M. Anciet Le Pors, was a Senator and a civil servant, and was made Minister for the civil service and for administrative reform. M.J. Ralite was a writer for *L'Humanité* on culture and was a Deputy until he became Health Minister and M.M. Rigout was a Communist Resistance member who was made Minister for Professional training. All the Communist Ministers have behaved impeccably so far and have kept Cabinet solidarity as team members.

Despite the 'sweetener' of four Ministry posts, it might be thought that the PCF would indulge in heart-searching reappraisal. Not so. Communists who attempted to open up the debate within the Party with a journal *Rencontres Communistes* were expelled (30, including the egregious Fizbin) and the PCF organisation was kept under firm control in the run-up to the 24th Congress in 1982. As far as an explanation for the Party's failures goes the Central Committee produced a resolution which underlined the PCF's errors from 1956-1976 and the common programme which had favoured the Left at Communist expense. Marchais, by contrast, was quite correct not to give in during the period of Left polemic and the report implicitly blamed Thorez and Waldeck Rochet for the PCF's current difficulties. Moreover the document warned the workers against hopes which could be dashed and against the (Socialist) system of currents which is a caricature of democracy, just as it eulogised the Eastern bloc and called for collaboration with other 'Socialist' countries.

The PCF was still closing down on its organisation a point emphasised by the replacement of Séguy by the hardliner Krasucki at the head of the CGT unions and the increased Communist hold on the union apparatus. Communists, like the Right, are waiting for the failure of the Socialist experiment so that they can recoup their recent losses. Thus, for example, the Communists in the Assembly debate on the property tax in November 1981 made their reservations clear: Parfait Jans *(sic)* stated that the tax was but an 'empty sack' and that the Socialists were too 'liberal'.

French Communism has not yet overcome the confusion of their defeat in the 1981 elections. Although Georges Marchais declared that nobody would be expelled from the Party (and nobody was during the mid-1970s when dissent and argument was allowed to flourish inside the PCF), there were exclusions and blacklistings as the presidential elections approached. Within the Party there was considerable dislike of the 1981 election strategy which effectively repudiated Left union, which imposed Marchais as presidential candidate, and which developed an increasingly anti-Socialist tone. Many Communists repudiated their Party in return (though some did so whilst claiming to remain true Communists) and there was a loss of party workers.

Since 1981, and despite the presence of four Communist Ministers in government, Communism has not revived either in numbers of activists or in votes. The Party declined to enter candidates for the by-elections of early 1982 and its 24th Congress did nothing to clarify the position. However the Party did use its CGT unions to play upon the difficulties which the government was experiencing even though this too failed to meet a positive response from the French workers who had just voted the Socialists into power. Nevertheless, there are no indications that the PCF intends either to relax its internal discipline, to break with Moscow, to re-admit dissidents or to return to the mid-1970s strategy of Left union.

Footnotes

1. See E. Mortimer (ed.), *Eurocommunism,* Penguin, 1979.
2. See D. Ligou, *Histoire du Socialisme en France,* Paris, 1962.
3. E. Dolléans, *Histoire du Mouvement ouvrier, 1830 à nos jeurs,* Paris, 1954 and G. Walker *Histoire du Parti Communiste Francais,* Paris, 1948.
4. For a concise discussion of this period see A. Cobban, *A History of Modern France,* (Vol. III), Penguin, 1965, pp.146-157.
5. A. Cobban *Ibid.*
6. A Werth, *The Twilight of France, 1933-40,* London, 1942.
7. Val Lorwin, *The French Labour movement,* Harvard UP, 1954.
8. See P.M. Williams, *Crisis and Compromise, London, 1964.*
9. *G.E. Elgey, La Republique des Illusions,* Paris, 1965, p.18 ff and V. Auriol *Journal du Septennat,* Paris, 1970, p.539 ff.
10. See A. Horne, *Algieria: Savage War of Peace,* Penguin, 1979.

11. See John Frears, *Political Parties and Elections in the French Republic,* Charles Hurst, 1977.
12. Charles Micaud, *Communism and the French Left,* Praeger, 1963.
13. D. Johnston, *The French Commun ist Party and the Students,* Yale, 1969.
14. *L'Ouvrier Francais en 1970* by G. Adam and F. Bon, Paris, A. Colin, 1970.
15. R. Tiersky, *French Communism 1920-1972,* Colombia UP, 1974.
16. R.L. Tökes (ed), *Eurocommunism and Detente,* New York Up, 1974. Ch.III for a sceptical interpretation.
17. Ian Campbell, 'The French Communists and the Union of the Left', in *Parliamentary Affairs,* Summer 1976, pp.246-63.

CHAPTER TWO

French Communism in the 1980s

THE COMMUNIST PARTY — ELECTORS AND MEMBERS

The PCF polled its best results in the Fourth Republic (1945-58) when in 1956 it averaged over 25 per cent of the vote, and when it was both the largest and best organised political force in the country. It sank deep roots in heavily industrialised areas like the North of France and the working class suburbs around Paris as well as in traditional left-wing bastions in the south like the agricultural Limousin and Languedoc.

In the first elections of the Fifth Republic, in 1958, the party suffered major losses. Large numbers of former supporters deserted it for the Gaullists and it gained only 19 per cent of the vote. Subsequently, it recouped some of these losses but failed to repair all the damage. Table One (below) gives details of the Communist voting record in the Fifth Republic.

Table One:
Communist Vote in Fifth Republic Elections

1958	18.9%
1962	21.8%
1967	22.5%
1968	20.0%
1969*	21.5%
1973	21.3%
1978	20.6%
1981*	15.3%
1982	16.2%

Presidentials

As can be seen from the table, Communist performance varied only slightly at each election until 1981. This indicates that it possessed a stable core of support. Nevertheless, it was consistently doing less well than in the years of the Fourth

Republic. Furthermore, the figures show from 1958-1978 a slight, but unmistakable waning of support. (This is particularly apparent if one recalls that the elections of 1968 were held in the exceptional circumstances of the aftermath of the May Events when the Gaullists swept all before them).

In 1978, the Communist vote was marginally down in nearly all parts of France. But the leadership breathed a sigh of relief: they had feared much larger losses. Anxiety had been fed by opinion poll findings which reported that the Communist electorate was falling to about 15 per cent of the total — at a time when the Left as a whole was prospering. Not only were the Socialists reaping all the benefits of the swing to the Left, but evidence also suggested that they were making inroads into the Communist working class base. These fears came true in 1981 when the Party did fall to 15 per cent.

There were many reasons for the collapse of the Union of the Left. Without a doubt, one of them was electoral. In the past, the Communists have always been the main beneficiaries when the Left has presented a united front — whether in the Popular Front of 1936, or the electoral alliance of 1967. This time, things were different. In the five years since the Common Programme had been signed, Communist leaders saw the revitalised Socialist Party forge ahead whilst their Party stayed behind in the backwaters. In 1972 Mitterrand had called for a "rebalancing of the Left": by 1981 the Socialists had so far succeeded that for every two Communists (according to the polls) there were three Socialists. Marchais and his colleagues had not signed the common programme to enable the Socialists to overtake their Party as the strongest force on the Left for the first time in 40 years.

One related fact was especially disturbing. As mentioned above, the French electoral system allows for two rounds. Unless one candidate wins the first round outright with 51 per cent, a second ballot has to be held. Electoral agreements between the PCF and the PS permitted 'Left-wing primaries' at the first round. Whichever party came out ahead would receive the support of the weaker Party on the second ballot. Now if (as opinion polls throughout 1977 recorded) the gap between the two partners grew too wide, then Socialist

candidates would move out ahead in the large majority of
Left-wing constituencies. In that event, Communist
candidates would have to withdraw at the second ballot in
favour of the Socialists, far more of whom would thereby be
elected and this is what happened in 1981. This problem was
exacerbated for the PCF by the slacker discipline of Socialist
voters. Whilst the great bulk of first-round Communists
could be relied upon to transfer their votes to a Socialist
candidate on the second ballot, only two-thirds of Socialist
voters have showed themselves willing to back a Communist
in the same circumstances.

If the polls had been proved right in 1978, and the Union of
the Left had held, the PCF might have found itself a junior
partner of the Socialists — a declining electoral force, and
one under-represented in Parliament at that. Once the
Communist leadership had decided to break the Union, they
threw the considerable weight of the Party machine behind a
determined campaign to win back former supporters tempted
by the PS. In areas where the two erstwhile allies were of
roughly equal strength (and, thus, where either might take
the lead on the first ballot) the PCF concentrated its fire on
its rival on the left, not on its enemy on the Right.

The results shown that in 1978 it was precisely in these
areas that the Communist vote held steady, or even rose
slightly. Thus, in many seats where in 1978 the Socialists
expected to out-poll the PCF on the first ballot, they failed to
do so. Whereas the former obtained a considerable number
of new votes, but won few new seats, the latter gained seats
whilst seeing their level of support slip back.

If the 1978 elections were a holding operation for the PCF
the 1981 elections were a definite setback. In 1978 the
Communists appeared to be hold 'their' 20 per cent of the
electorate against the Socialist Party and the same seemed
true in 1979 but in 1981 decline of the PCF candidate's vote
to 15.34 per cent (4,456,922) was one of the main features of
the election. Marchais attributed this to the 'joint efforts of
the Right and the Socialist Party' but his own campaign —
though very energetic — did not seem to produce results.
Beside the Socialist gains the problem is whether this is a
historic trend or merely the result of the elections of 1981.

In the Presidential elections Georges Marchais lost in

working class areas and its own fiefdoms. Relative to 1978 and 1979 the stagnation of the PCF vote in some areas and its decline in industrial areas and (for European elections) its slight increase in rural areas gave way to decline in all areas except Haute-Corse and Lozère where miniscule increases were registered (0.26 per cent and 0.07 per cent respectively). Communist votes fell heavily in some industrial areas like the Nord, Lorraine and the Bouches-du-Rhône.

In the Paris region, long considered to be a Communist stronghold, (the red belt) the Communists lost 10.69 per cent in Seine-Saint-Denis, and in Paris itself it lost 6.43 per cent. Other areas where the PCF lost heavily were Seine-Maritime (9 per cent) the Marne (8.71 per cent) and in the agricultural areas of Gord (8.65 per cent), Pyrénées-Orientales (6.3 per cent), Vaucluse (6 per cent) and its biggest loss was 12.75 per cent in the Cher. This last area is an agricultural district of small industry where the PCF has long been dug-in but it did manage to hold on to its vote rather better in Longuedoc-Roussillon and Provence where the party still benefits from anti-Europeanism. The party held its vote best in areas where it had a tiny sect-like existence on the margins of serious politics (Alsace and the West) and the beneficiaries of the party's decline were M. Mitterrand and to a small extent the Trotskyists.

The French Communist Party's poor showing on the first ballot of the presidential elections left it in no position to bargain with the Socialists over the transfer of votes on the second. Thus the disappearance of the Communist 'threat' was hugely beneficial to Mitterrand's campaign for the floating vote. Communist votes transferred well to Mitterrand on the second ballot but there were a few hints of reservations about the Socialists in some PCF areas. As a result of the first and second ballots of the presidential elections the PCF ceased to be the main working class party in France.

In May 1981 the legislative elections were a vote for the new president's party, a wave of sympathy for the Left from which the PCF did not benefit despite having campaigned as an integral and loyal part of the Left prior to the legislative ballots. On the first round the PCF polled 16.12 per cent hardly an improvement on Marchais' 15.34 per cent and well down on 1978's 20.61 per cent. More importantly, in the number of winnable seats the Communists were ahead in only 65 out of 489 seats (the total was 144). This meant that the PCF candidate had to stand down for the Socialist in many favourable areas. In this way well-known Communist figures fell throughout the country: Maxime Gremetz (Somme), Paul Laurent (Paris 29), Georges Lazzarino (Bouches-de-Rhône 5), Roland Leroy (Seine-Maritime 3), Gisèle Moreau (Paris 13), Marcel Tassy (Bouches-du-Rhône 8) etc. In all 46 of the 87 outgoing PCF Deputies were displaced and only seven seats were won by the PCF on the first ballot.

Communists were on the downgrade in almost all departments in all regions but the spectacular last minute swing to the support of the Socialists may have accounted for the slight revival in percentage vote. The PCF candidates very often did not present themselves as 'Communist' but rather emphasised that they were the 'outgoing deputy'.

Relative to the presidential election the PCF increased its vote in a few departments such as Alpes-de-Haute-Provence and maintained its vote relative to 1978 in a few like Saint-Denis, Haute-Vienne, Corrège and Val-d'Oise. However the progress of the PCF from Marchais' poll in the presidential elections was offset by a fall in the vote in the rest — Communists held on better where there was a 1978 PCF Deputy. This was particularly striking in Paris where the PCF had seven Deputies in 1978 they kept none in 1981 because they were beaten by Socialists and the party's vote fell to 9.36 per cent (the presidential vote had been 9.18 per cent PCF in Paris). Set against this was the Socialist progress to 30.62 per cent.

Following the lead of the presidential elections the Socialists won extensively in the Paris suburbs where only Hautes-de-Seine resisted the Socialist breakthrough. (The eleven Communist Deputies defeated on the first round here were beaten by Socialists). The ability of the Socialists to defeat the PCF candidates on the first round won them numerous seats because the Socialists were always more capable of beating the Right than were Communists who were not attractive to the floating voter.

The results on the second round were no better for the PCF which lost half of its Assembly seats and now has only 44 and its bastions were penetrated by the Socialist Party. Only one of the 37 candidates it put up in France was defeated (in Alpes-Maritimes) on the second ballot and Communist discipline was exemplary in transfers to Socialists on the second ballot (although the Socialist transfers to PCF candidates were not so good). Thus the second ballot in May confirmed Communist losses in the presidentials and also underlined Socialist domination over the PCF.

Nevertheless, in one area, there were signs of movement from the Communists to their competitors on the Left. In the Paris region, where the Communits had dominated Left-wing politics for four decades, they fell back from 27.1 per cent to 24.2 per cent of the poll in 1978 and to 9.18 per cent in 1981. (In 1967 they had notched up 30 per cent). In contrast, the non-Communist Left (which had secured only 12.4 per cent in 1967) continued to progress, reaching 21 per cent of the total. Communists also lost seats (and, in several constituencies their leading place on the first round) to the Socialists.

How does the Communist electorate differ from the Socialist one? Firstly, it is more proletarian. 36 per cent of all working class electors backed the Communists in 1978, compared to 27 per cent for the Socialists (and 31 per cent for the Right).[1] 47 per cent of all Communist voters work in manual occupations. A larger proportion belong to the working class, (French electoral statistics include the category of the 'inactive and retired', of which a fair number must be former workers).The proportion for the Socialists is 30 per cent.[2] It also enjoys the support of 18 per cent of white collar workers (29 per cent for the Socialists). Unlike the PS, it has made no gains amongst church-going Catholics; its voters are overwhelmingly either non-practising Catholics or without any religious affiliation.

The PCF pursued a purely negative strategy for the 1978 and 1981 elections — to hold on to their existing level of support. In this, they were not successful. Moreover, its electoral prospects for the future can hardly be deemed bright. It has demonstrated once more that it possesses a solid bedrock of support — but also that (unlike, say, the Italian Communist Party) it has very limited capacity to win fresh adherents. Social groups, like white collar workers, technicians and so forth, which constitute a growing proportion of the electorate, and offer a likely source of converts to the Left, have shown that they prefer the Socialist to the Communist Party. Similarly, in historically Conservative regions which are swinging to the Left, it is the former which is making the running whilst the latter stagnates.

To conclude that the future is bleak for the PCF is, however, misleading. It possesses access to non-electoral resources on a scale denied to the PS. Its membership is much larger — possibly more than three times that of the Socialists (although there is considerable turnover in PCF activists): about half of these are manual workers, a much higher percentage than for the Socialists. The membership is also much better organised and more highly disciplined. Furthermore, the largest and most efficiently organised trade union federation, the CGT, remains solidly under Communist control. As a force for mobilising support and inspiring activity (both industrial and political) the Communist machine remains far more impressive than the Socialist as demonstrations against nuclear warfare in Paris in October 1981 seem to show. Moreover the Communist Party is waiting for the opportunity to profit from Socialist mistakes or a deterioration in the economy.

CURRENTS WITHIN THE COMMUNIST PARTY

Although the closed nature of Party organisation makes it exceptionally difficult to say what the different currents are inside the PCF at any time, it is clear that French Communism is crossed by movements of opinion and disagreements within the leadership. In the 1970s these have tended to be represented in the outside press as 'Eurocommunism for and against' but this is probably a distortion of the true state of affairs.

For the union of the Left in France the most important split appears to have been the mid-1970s disagreements over the strategy of alliance with the Socialists. This dispute burst on an otherwise tranquil scene at the meeting of the political bureau in October 1974 just after the eventful election campaign by Mitterrand in which he (as the Left's common candidate) polled some 13 million votes. Georges Marchais seems to have been taken aback by the hostility within the Party to the Socialist/Communist alliance and he appears to have been under personal attack from certain sections. The campaign seems to have been whipped up by Roland Leroy — Marchais' long-time rival — who distrusted the relationship with the Socialists in which some thought that the Communists were losers.[3]

Some commentators have seen the hand of Moscow in the 1974 split because the Russians were always suspicious of Left union in France. However Roland Leroy is no pro-Russian and a more likely explanation is that within the Party there was an alliance between the pro-Soviet old guard (still strong) and an anti-Marchais group which basically disliked the strategy of Left union. This leadership split triggered off the polemic with the Socialists and came hard on the heels of by-election results which were, to some, indications of the Socialist gains and Communist losses (or stagnation) as a result of Left union.

Georges Marchais associated himself both with Left union and liberalisation within the Party but had not noticed that opposition to these policies had been building up and had been encouraged by Leroy. 'Liberal' Communism therefore suffered a setback as did the Marchais group a fact underlined by the peculiar hard-line Vitry-sur-Seine 1974 extraordinary congress at which the Party line took a U-turn back to a policy of open hostility to the Socialist Party. However Marchais, adopting the tactic of *fuite en avant,* became the Party spokesman for attacks on the Socialists while at the same time campaigning to regain control of the Party leadership. Marchais was helped by the fall in popularity sufferred by the Socialist Party as a result of Communist attacks but he had also run a barn-storming campaign in the provinces to bring the hardliners to heel. This seems to have been confirmed by the meeting in April 1975 of the PCF's Central Committee at which 'liberal' themes were re-emphasised though not without noting the need for eternal vigilance over the Socialists. Probably because of persistent pressure in the party the leadership could not go back, even had it wanted to, to the peaceful collaboration with the Socialists of the 1973-74 period.

Communist Party opening out appeared to have been

confirmed by the 'Eurocommunist' 22nd Congress of the PCF in February 1976 (celebrated in phrase and fable) and Marchais' position at the head of the Party has been assured. Although Marchais' opponents have steadily been demoted and the Secretariat filled with his own nominees the Party retains its suspicion of the Socialists inaugurated in September 1974 and presumably retains sizeable anti-Socialist Party and pro-Soviet groups.[4]

A split within the Party which has, paradoxically gained more publicity but probably been less important is the post-1978 election dissent of intellectuals, most of them inspired by the prospect of a 'liberal' (Italianate) PCF opened up by the 22nd Congress. Past Communist Party relationships with intellectuals have not always been easy but if the party was pleased to have the prestige of association with Picasso or Curie they were not the prime concern and were, in the last resort, expendable. There have been several attempts to bring the intellectual sector under control but there has been a persistent tendency for intellectuals to escape control. In mid-1966 the Argenteuil Central Committee meeting tried to set the party/intellectual relationship on a more open basis but there have been persistent crises which have included the expulsion of Roger Garaudy and, in 1981, the effective exclusion of 30 dissident intellectuals who formed a group called *Recontres Communistes.*

Yet the current crisis in the Party stems from other sources than this persistent grumbling. Communist intellectuals seem to have mistakenly taken the 22nd Congress as a sign that the PCF was begining to move in a direction similar to the Italian Communists and, at the very least, that they would have a liberty to write about the Party line critically both within and outside the Party press.

Jean Elleinstein, in particular, was representative of the 'new' Communism inaugurated by the 22nd Congress and for a long time wrote with a freedom and outspokenness which can only have been licensed from above. Among the books which Elleinstein wrote was one on the party itself and one on the *Stalinist Phenomenon.* These two books illustrate the scope and limits of the 'Eurocommunism' of the 22nd Congress for they represent a groping in the dark rather than a new certainty. For example the book on Stalinism was a

recognition of what 'bourgeois' history had long known —
the dictatorial nature of the East — but brought nothing new
to the appreciation of the Eastern bloc. However it did
represent a Communist recognition that there was such a
thing as Stalinism although it managed to avoid giving any
real consideration of what the role of the Communist Party
was in Stalin's crimes.[5]

More difficult for intellectuals in the party to come to
terms with was the collapse of Left union in the legislative
elections of 1978 and the PCF's sabotage of the Left's hopes
by the PCF. This unleashed a series of criticisms of the
party's internal structure and recent anti-Left union line.
Jean Elleinstein made one comment in *Le Monde* appealing
for a more 'liberal' party but without giving any hope that
this could be achieved and poor Louis Althusser (the party's
most eminent philosopher) wrote another series of *Le Monde*
articles which were extremely obscure but in which he
appeared to take the view that inner-party democracy ought
to be introduced to an extent. Althusser has since recanted
this daring view whereas Elleinstein appears to have been
nicely isolated, others have voted with their feet by leaving
but there remains considerable discontent in intellectual
ranks at the closing of the 22nd Congress' openings as
evidenced by the difficulties in slapping down the Paris
Federation which was headed by Henri Fizbin who like
Elleinstein has since been expelled.

Internal Party differences only serve to emphasise the
continuing importance of democratic centralism in the PCF.
As long as this form of Party discipline continues the
possibility of a closing down or complete reversal of policy is
very much present. Ironicaly the 'liberal' line of the 22nd
Congress was made possible by the iron rule of democratic
centralism which imposed the new ideas on the Party and
enabled 'unanimous' rejection of the notion of 'dictatorship
of the proletariat'. French Communism has been careful to
guard the discipline of democratic centralism even while
opening out in other fields and in this it is to be distinguished
from the Italian and Spanish Communists where open debate
is possible. So far, therefore, intellectual dissidence remains
so much froth on the surface although different deep-
running, conflicting, currents occasionally come into view.

FRENCH COMMUNISM AND THE USSR

As the well known saying has it 'French Communism is neither of the Left nor the Right but of the East'. This sums up the relationship that the French Communist Party has had with the Soviet Union through most of its existence, when it was proud of its position as the 'eldest daughter of the (Stalin) Church' and its leader described himself as the "foremost Stalinist in France"; the relationship has been one of master and willing servant.[6]

Yet the French Communist servility towards Moscow has undergone some changes in the 1970s although the roots of these painful shifts of poicy can be traced back further to Maurice Thorez, Jacques Duclos and Benoît Franchon who kept French Communism behind Stalin throughout the '30s and '40s and no doubt there would have been no signs of independence from Moscow had Stalin lived as long as Tito. But the rise of Khruschev to power and the slight liberalising of Moscow policy led the hardline Stalinist PCF leadership, if not to question Russian wisdom, at least to ask for explanations. For a short time with Khruschev in charge of Russian policy and Thorez as secretary-general of the PCF the French Communists were more royal than the king in their emphasis on loyalty to Stalin's old policies — the PCF refused to refer to Khruschev's criticism of Stalin, for example.

French Communists supported the Russian invasion of Hungary and the Party remained loyal to Moscow's policy priorities although it began increasingly to think of its own interests first. Thus when Waldeck-Rochet became secretary-general in 1964 after Thorez' death French Communist relations with Moscow began to shift because Moscow supported de Gaulle and because the strategy of Left union (endorsed by the Party's 17th Congress) demanded that the Party display its independence of foreign control. However the practical application of this newly felt need for independence was very slow, the Party was founded on faith in the USSR as *the* Socialist experiment and loyalty to Moscow was deeply ingrained in French Communism.

Hints of PCF independence came in the mid-1960s when, for example, the Party newspaper *l'Humanité* was seized in Russia after criticisms of the trial of the Russian dissidents

Sinyavsky and Daniel but these incidents were few and far between. When the Russians invaded Dubcek's Czechoslovakia in 1968 the French Communist reaction was to express 'surprise and reprobation' but although the Party condemned the invasion it gradually moved to support subsequent Soviet actions including 'normalisation' and the Husak regime. Hence the original condemnation was subsequently qualified out of existence presumably as a result of intense Russian pressure.

French Communists expressed reservations about certain aspects of Russian and Eastern European policy in the early 1970s once the pressures of the Czech invasion had decreased but they were not a recognition of any deep malaise in 'Socialist' societies. Instead the PCF occasionally reacted to events such as the Gdansk riots in Poland or the Russian Ambassador's visit to Giscard in the middle of the 1974 elections by specific and limited comments about societies which were still officially described as 'Socialist'.

The two years 1975-1976 are a significant break in the long history of PCF adulation of the USSR and represent a distinctive autonomy associated with the discussion of 'Eurocommunism' during this period. French Communists during this period began to make a number of serious criticisms of the Soviet Union and its satellites going beyond anything expressed before. A newly discovered interest in human rights meant that the PCF took the 'Socialist states' to task for their abuse of liberties and the penal system of the East. These criticisms were reactive, as if the party had discovered for the first time that such practices existed in the East, and they were responses to complaints about particular injustices. French Communists did not take up issues or espouse causes, they replied to well-known problems. Nevertheless this was considerable progress for the party particularly when combined with the concession that these were not mere superficial miscarriages of justice. But for the PCF the East was still 'Socialist'; their attitude was not one of complete rejection because this word is the most prized of all labels in the Communist lexicon.[7]

Another aspect of the 1975-1976 period was the severance of formal contacts with the Soviet Union. Previous French Communists have felt the need for constant contact with (and approval from) the USSR but in the mid-1970s the PCF did cut these links in a show of independence. There were therefore the November 1975 refusal to reaffirm 'proletarian internationalism' at the Pan-European Communist Conference, the non-attendance at the 25th Soviet Party Congress, the party's independence at the East Berlin Conference of June 1976, and the PCF's use of the name 'Eurocommunist' as applied to itself (this was condemned by Moscow).

French Communists also entered into bi-lateral relations with other West European CPs — notably the Italians and Spanish — in the mid-1970s in a way which they had not done previously. One aspect of this was what the outside world called 'Eurocommunism' to describe the convergence between Spanish, Italian and French Communists to underline their own independence. These meetings included the Madrid summit of March 1977 but no 'Eurocommunist' view as such appeared from the three parties and, largely at French insistence, they refrained from appearing to 'gang up' against the USSR by publicly condemning the Russians. As important were the bi-lateral French-Italian meetings which inaugurated PCI-PCF relations although in the past the two parties were on notoriously bad terms the Italians representing 'polycentrism' and the French 'Moscow hegemony'. With the Spanish Communist Party relations have tended to be more distant than with the Italians because the PCE has been rather more 'liberal' than the PCF.

Since 1977 the PCF's relations to the USSR has changed once again. This change probably came as a result of the collapse of the union of the Left in France and no doubt includes the pressures consequent on the colder international climate. A rapprochement with the Russians was permitted by the Communist decision to pursue a stragegy of isolation in French domestic politics as evidence by the startling announcement by the PCF in 1979 that the balance sheet for the Eastern Socialist countries was 'generally positive'. This ambiguous formula probably represents a concession to Stalinists within the Party but it must be noted that the PCF has continued to condemn the violation of human rights in the East so that it is not a case of one step forward and two back but of slight advances.[8]

More important on the international level was the PCF's clear defence of the USSR's invasion of Afghanistan. Significantly Georges Marchais chose to make this defence while actually in Moscow on an official Party visit and repeated it over a live TV link to the French public. The arguments advanced in defence of this action are more or less a repetition of Moscow's: the Afghanistan government was threatened by 'feudal' subversives organised by the Americans out of Pakistan and all the Russians did was to come to the defence of the legitimate government once its aid had been requested. Parroting such arguments sets the PCF apart from the PCI and PCE who have condemned the Russian invasion but it is more than just a superficial point because the French Communist Party has espoused the view that the world is still divided into two camps (the imperialist West and Socialist East) and a choice has to be made for the Soviet side. Spanish and Italian Communists refuse this dichotomy and continue to assert that European independence of such forced choices is still possible.

This polarisation of the Communist world and the PCF decision to support the Eastern bloc was demonstrated when the French Party organised a conference for world peace in Paris at the end of April 1980. This conference was set up at the behest of the Russians by the joint French and Polish Parties but it was not attended by the independent Communist Parties of Spain, Italy or Romania. The final resolution which was fairly anodyne, recognised (which is in fact significant inside the Communist world) Communist differences but re-emphasised the importance of world peace and the aggressive American attitude (in particular US nuclear policy).

French Communists, it is probably true to say, are no longer controlled by Moscow. Yet they continue to place a very high value on Russian demands and are very much attuned to Russian interests. This is the position at the end of a long PCF road towards French Left union which seemed to be taking them further and further from the USSR. It does not seem to be the case that the PCF has been forced back onto the Russian road by external pressures. Rather it is more likely that the collapse of the Left in France in 1978 allowed French Communism to return to old certainties.

French Communism may be subservient to Moscow but this should not be exaggerated for the Party retains its links with the PCI and has not reneged on its muted criticisms of human rights violations in the East. The problem is that these small victories could be reversed if internal French Communist politics demand it and there is very little evidence for the optimist who wishes to believe in a continuation of the mid-1970s 'liberal' evolution.[9]

COMMUNIST/SOCIALIST RELATIONS IN FRANCE

Relations on the Left have been far from fraternal for the most part of post-war history. Communists and Socialists have been divided by numerous disagreements on principle stemming from the fact that the PCF was a totalitarian Party tied to the foreign policy demands formulated by the Russian government in Moscow. Socialists and Communists fought an ideological (and sometimes physical) battle for the soul of the French Left through the Fourth Republic into the 1960s and, except for a short period from 1972-74, it has hardly abated. However before the advent of the new Socialist Party the quarrel turned on the classical issues of whether the PCF would stand down from power if the Left was defeated in elections, on whether the PCF was the only party of the Left, and relations with the USSR and USA.

These problems were not completely solved during the 1960s but they were shelved to the extent that a Communist/Socialist rapprochement became possible. French Communists decided to participate in the national political system and made advances to the Socialists so that an alliance could be formed enabling a Communist presence — of some unspecified sort — on the French political stage. French Communists made a number of concessions which satisfied Socialist criteria for democratic politics. Thus the notion of *parti unique* was abandoned and acceptance of *alternance* (i.e. readiness to vacate office if defeated at the polls) was made clear although other areas of ambiguity were left untackled.

Throughout the 1960s Communist tactics could be seen as an attempt to persuade the divided, weak, uncertain, and hesitant Socialists to join the PCF in Left union on the basis of a common programme of government for a future legislature. Socialists were understandably chary of this large disciplined machine-like organisation whose de-Stalinisation had been remarkably tardy and their reactions ranged from the 'wait and see' to the 'never on any condition'. Neither Socialists nor Communists seem to have countenanced the possibility of a rapid growth of the non-Communist Left and neither seems to have given much thought to the mechanics of co-operation in government or in policy-making in a consolidated Left.

All these considerations were at some remove in 1969 when the Communists, victorious from Jacques Duclos' good election showing, and the Socialists, suffering an electoral humiliation, were working out the background to an agreement. When Mitterrand became leader of the Socialist Party in 1971 he was committed to finding an agreement with the PCF for a common programme and continuing the electoral deal. French Socialism had recovered considerably but it was still very weak relative to the PCF and the common programme in 1972 was negotiated from weakness.

In coming to an electoral agreement plus the common programme Communists and Socialists had gone further down the road to Left unity than even the Popular Front of 1936. But problems remained. What would be the division of responsibility in a future government? Any 50-50 division which reflected relative electoral strength, would frighten floating voters but, more to the point, what would happen to key ministries such as defence, Treasury, Foreign Affairs etc? Would Communists accept minor posts? Then there was the interpretation of the common programme: there was no settled reading of the document. Socialists and Communists had different views from the start. Moreover would Socialists stick to the letter of the programme? It was negotiated from Socialist weakness, so when the balance of forces changed would the Socialists accept it?

The last point is particularly crucial because Mitterrand's strategy meant that the Socialists would first seek an alliance with the PCF then try to capture the floating voter. But the floating voter was notoriously wary of the Communists and not interested in the Socialist logic of the common programme. Mitterrand was to drive this point home to Communists in his presidential campaign of 1974 which made only perfunctionary references to the common programme and which was studiously moderate.

There were also changes of domestic and international conditions after the common programme agreement of 1972, most notably the onset of the world recession which began to hit France in 1974. It was one thing for the common programme to promise Japanese-style growth in the early seventies and another after the onset of recession. Furthermore sharing out an expanding cake is a different thing to organising austerity policy and this dilemma opened out a series of disagreements between Socialist and Communist economists.

Seeds of potential disagreement were buried within the Left-wing of 1972 but as long as the Communist Party remained the largest component of the Left and so long as the Socialist Party posed no real threat to traditional Communist dominance they remained mere potential. However after 1974 it became clear that the Socialist Party was growing disproportionately. The realisation that the Socialists and not the Communists were gaining from Left unity and the possibility that Socialists were even gaining Communist votes started the polemic of the Left (described above) which has not yet abated.

Many commentators have seen the Socialist/Communist quarrel as a result of Communist distaste at discovering that their position as 'first Party of the Left' had been undermined. It is probably more complicated than this. Communists were certainly annoyed at increasing Socialist influence but they were also annoyed at what they saw as the Socialist abandonment of the clear Socialist programme negotiated in 1972. In other words the Communist Party was not prepared to come to power at any price and if the cost of electoral victory (as the Mitterrand group appeared to believe) was a non-Socialist weakly reformist government acceptable to the floating voters then the 'victory' was a false one and certainly not worth the price. To this can be added the question of what a Socialist-led government would do when faced with the recession. For the PCF the Socialists' answers were not convincing since Communists had made plain since the onset of the recession that they were not prepared to come to power to force an incomes policy or a policy of austerity on their own supporters. (This parallels the Communist/Socialist fights in 1947).

Hence for a multitude of reasons the Socialist/Communist relationship soured after 1974. Too many questions were left open by the Common Programme of 1972 for the alliance to survive a change in the balance of power and a change in economic climate. Moreover with the polemic continuing until the eve of the 1978 elections mutual recriminations grew worse and bitterness increased. Communists accused Socialists of sabotaging the re-negotiation of the Common Programme in the autumn of 1977 (and vice versa) and the argument became increasingly abstruse except that a fundamental incompatibility clearly remained.[10]

After the 1978 elections the Communist Party moved into isolation. Clearly determined to cultivate its own cabbage patch, the PCF has turned its back on its own policy of the last twenty years of Left union.[11] A vigorous polemic with the Socialists continued until the elections of 1981, although the bulk of the Socialist Party around Mitterrand clearly hoped that the PCF would come to its senses and revive the union of the Left.

On the one hand the Socialists are hoping that the pressures will further build up on the Communist Party (these have already been evident in its declining vote, departing activists, dissidence and loss of support) and the PCF will have to move back towards the Socialists. Mitterrand believed that his party could ensure this by maintaining the policies which brought it success in the elections of 1981.[12] On the other hand the Communists seem to believe that by keeping its Ministers in the Socialist government and by increasing the pressures on the Socialist Party, Mitterrand's experiment will fail to the benefit of the PCF. Both the major parties on the Left are therefore assuming that the other will split or fall apart or crumble under persistent pressure if they pursue their own implacable course without making concessions. Communists are betting on Socialist government failure and Socialists are betting on an even greater Communist collapse. It could be that both will be right or both wrong or, what is more likely, they could be destroying the prospect of a Left-wing Republic.

Footnotes

1. V. Wright *op.cit.* p.39.
2. *Le Matin Dossier*, Legislative Elections 1978, pp.38, 86.
3. John Frears, *op.cit.*
4. See Vincent Wright, *The Government and Politics of France*, Hutchinson, 1978 (Chapter on the Left).
5. H. Weber (ed.) *Changer le PC*, Paris, 1979.
6. Anne Kriegel *Un autre Communisme*, Paris, 1978.
7. Colette Ysmal 'PC et les raisons d'un durcissement' *Project*, January 1979, No.121, pp.45-54.
8. C. Ysmal 'Une nonvelle strategre pour le PCF' *Project*, April, 1975.
9. P. Robrieux 'Le PCF et l'union de la gauche' *La Nouvelle Revue Socialiste*, (Special edn. 1976).
10. *Le Matin*, May 15, 1979.
11. *Le Matin*, March 7, 1980.
12. *Le Matin*, February 12, 1980.

CHAPTER THREE

The Communist Party's Organisation and Doctrine

PARTY ORGANISATION

In the long history of disagreements between Communists and Socialists the issue of organisation has consistently set the Moscow oriented parties apart from others on the Left. Until recently all the Leninist Parties of the Third (Moscow) International were alike in this respect but the Spanish and Italian Communist organisations have loosened up a good deal. It is the formidably strong disciplined, cast-like interior structure which makes the PCF a 'party unlike the others' so this aspect requires careful investigation because it is important in French Communism and for the French Left.

Party organisation in the PCF retains the old Leninist features. It is based on cell units and works according to the classic rules of democratic centralism. The cells are small groups of five or so Communists in geographical or workplace units. All members must belong to a cell (this is not the case in Spain's Communist Party) and great emphasis is put on the cells in factories and offices for the workplace cell enhances the extra-parliamentary capability of the Party, its presence and leadership in industrial disputes, and its continued organised presence at the heart of the working class. Not all of these workplace cells will be in industrial working class areas, there are numerous middle class cells in schools, offices, etc., but the Party claims to have some 8,000 or so workplace cells. In addition there are associated Communist groups such as the sixth form school organisation UNCAL, the student's organisation, intellectual circles and so on. These supplement the cell structure and serve to keep an organised Communist presence in these fields.[1]

It is difficult to be precise about the membership of the PCF because the Party has been rather coy about the figures since the 1978 election débâcle and because it is difficult to know what the criteria are for being a 'member'. Nonetheless the Party organisation is immense, perhaps outstripping the nearest French rivals and the Labour Party for it claimed a 700,000 membership which could, in reality, be between 100,000 and 400,000. Membership is not cheap, although the tariff depends on whether you are unemployed or a millionaire (there are Communist millionaires), but it no longer seems to depend on regular attendance at cell meetings because you can buy one year's contribution at a single time — the regular monthly meeting to buy a new stamp for membership cards used to be part of PCF folklore.

What Communists do is simpler to describe. Party cells are responsible for a number of tasks like the pre-eminent duty of selling the Party products, the Sunday newspaper *l'Humanité Dimanche*, and the daily *l'Humanité* as well as other literature, the common programme in its Communist produced form, for example. Cells are also meant to make sure that Communist campaigns are made known through distribution of tracts or attendance at demonstrations but they also carry out the normal election tasks of putting up posters, canvassing (though not like the UK system), holding election meetings etc. Communists are the cart-horses of the Left and Mitterrand's 1965 and 1974 bids for the presidency depended a good deal on Communist willingness to carry out this sort of basic task.

There is a good deal of discussion at cell level and this is more or less open although a cell which continually causes trouble will receive a visit from a high-ranking Party official and if it proves to be refractory could well be dissolved. Expulsions seem to be a thing of the past and it is eight years or so since this measure was used to discipline somebody so in this sense the Marchais regime is more liberal, but being a persistent critic is not the way to progress in the PCF and exclusions have started again since 1980. A 1980 campaign by several cells simultaneously to have the PCF historian Jean Elleinstein expelled thus presaged a return to old ways but the campaign, although clearly organised from the top, was followed by a declaration that he had 'put himself outside the Party' — dissidents were, in effect, expelled.

Communist cells are not in contact with each other, there is no horizontal network of contacts across the party, the only communication is vertical and that comes from the base up. It is still a grave crime for Communists to express themselves in the 'bourgeois' press which meant that since the party controlled its own press, dissidents were unable to gain a hearing for views contrary to the current line but over the late 1970s it became frequent for Communists to write for the newspapers and write books — this is now a minor industry as PCF dissidents are highly articulate. The publication of *Recontres Communistes* by Fizbin et. al., which tried to organise dissident Communists led to 'expulsion'.

However the importance of cells and ordinary members are that they are the building blocks for the party, they are not the source of power within the party. Starting with the cells at the base, the next level is the Federation all presided over by the biennial national congress which elects the political bureau and Secretariat. But the relationship in fact works in reverse with commands coming down from the leadership which hence controls all aspects of party life. Communist activists have no way of making their voice felt in higher party organs: ordinary party members do not stay in the party to make their displeasure at certain policies clear, rather they simply leave. There is therefore no way, from the outside, of assessing the internal feeling which, anyway, will support the leadership, disgruntlement in the ranks shows up mainly in declining numbers and these are not public knowledge. Of course some areas, like the intellectual Paris Federation, will make a good deal of noise but this gives no gauge of opinion within the party. It should not be thought that PCF activists are a constant source of pressure on the leadership, they are there because they want to be and as such support the party. One further point on activists is that the party demands a very high commitment from cells so that members are quickly 'burnt out' and leave, a high turnover of supporters is thus normal in the PCF although there is a nucleus of stable dependables. It is this stable group of 'iron butts' with the ability to sit out interminable meetings and committees which forms the party's organisational backbone; continually renewed the party is hence always the same.[2]

None of the party activists' intense bustle is liable to

destroy the unity of the oarty for another reason: the organisational principle is democratic centralism. In other words the oarty is centralised but not democratic for the levels above that of the cell are nominated by the level above. There are elections in the PCF at Federation and National level but these are elections only in an Eastern European sense, that is to say, they are nominations by the leadership. Party national congresses are supposedly sovereign conferences but in fact they are hand picked cliques and therefore say something about the balance of power in the leadership but nothing about the party activists. Congresses are therefore more celebrations of Communist unity and Communist 'communions', not the decision-making bodies or debating assemblies found in Socialist parties.

Cells are grouped into regional sections and sections are organised into Departmental Federations (i.e. by county council unit). As the various Federations have different levels of activity and support the apparatus will not be quite the same in each but formally these Departmental organisations all have a Federal Secretary and a Political Bureau responsible for local business. Because of uneven Communist implantation Federations vary in size and importance from the enormous Nord and Marseilles to smaller ones and the Federal Secretary will be a powerful figure in the former cases.

Above the Federation is the national organisation which includes the ostensibly sovereign Congress which meets at least every three years and is composed of delegates from Federal congresses. At the Congress the Central Committee is chosen (or rather unveiled before the faithful, for there are not open elections) an organ of 21 members (and some substitute members). The Central Committee is suposed to survey party activity in the absence of the Congress but in fact power is held by the Political Bureau composed of some 21 members and this is where inner-party battles are fought out. As many have observed monolithic unity expressed as eulogistic approval of the current line are the role at other levels. P. Robrieux describes his speech to the Central Committee at which he defended his own action against the prevailing official view but he was flung out before he could repeat the experiment in party discussion.[3]

Within the Political Bureau is the smaller Secretariat presided over by the secretary-general. Relations between Political Bureau and Secretariat will change depending on whether (like Thorez) the leader has total control over the Party or (like Marchais in the mid-1970s) control is not complete. The tendency over the long-term is for the secretary-general to assert his authority through use of Party resources (particularly patronage) and for the leader to have a more or less complete sway over decisive issues. Georges Marchais may well be in that position of absolute power in the Party which characterised Maurice Thorez but it has been a long 10-year struggle and his very poor showing in the 1981 presidential election cannot have helped.

Thus French Communist organisation is therefore the classical hierarchical pyramid stuck together with the Leninist glue of democratic centralism which has so far proved resistant to the corrosive effects of post-war Western society.

This discipline can be seen in Communist meetings. Mass demonstrations and assemblies of party supporters are very much a part of French political life. Communists go in for a style of huge mass rally or meeting which has not been seen in this country since the 30s Olympia gatherings. These are, however, very effectively policed by the party *service d'ordre* (stewards) and *demos* by the CGT stewards; nevertheless they are occasions for the display of great emotion. High feeling among activists contrasts with the bureaucracy of the party and its Stalinist style. Leaders appear on a dias ranged (in their dark blue suits showing white cuffs) and read speeches for as much as three hours at a time. Champion in this league is Georges Marchais who has the ability to plough through texts but who can bring them to life. It is possible, on leaving a large Communist assembly, to buy a copy of *l'Humanité* (early edition) to follow the speaker as he reads the text relayed by loud speakers outside.

Bureaucracy is carried through to the rest of the Party life. French Communists have their own publishing company (Editions Sociales), some regional newspapers (*La Marseillaise,* for example), and it has other publications for the young, women, intellectuals and special sections of the French public. It also has a stake in many businesses and owns others though the extent — and efficiency — of much

of the Party's business activity is a matter of dispute just as is
the question of what it gets from Moscow nowadays. What is
not in dispute is the size of Communist interests in the
business world, these must be substantial. Communist central
headquarters in Paris are in a huge, specially designed, steel
and concrete building which is far beyond the means of any
bourgeois party. Rumours abound about this building, as
about other PCF activities, and it seems to be the case that all
sections of Party business are overseen by the massive
bureaucracy in Paris headquarters.

PARTY DOCTRINE

French Communists, like all orthodox Communists, adhere
to the theory of state monopoly capitalism. SMC is not
'theory' in any sohpisticated sense and its importance lies
more in what it excludes rather than what it predicts for it is
largely a tabulation of political demands. The theory is
supposedly a development of Lenin's ideas and was briefly
mentioned by Stalin so that the Communists are enabled to
claim to maintain direct links with previous theorists in SMC
discussion — it is also asserted to be a Marxist theory of
capitalism.

A Socialist system is seen as an SMC system which has been
wrested from the control of capitalist monopolies and which
is working in the interests of the exploited classes.[4]

Capitalism crises still occur but the growth of the system is
much greater than in the 19th century. Yet although new
mechanisms of economic control have been developed there
are still antagonistic contradictions and these will lead to the
impending collapse of the system because the state and
capital have become inter-twined. Capitalist states now
depend on the monopolies and *vice versa,* but they cannot
escape the ultimate self-destructive logic of the falling rate of
profit or over-accumulation — though what benefits the state
benefits the monopolies under SMC.[5]

Until recently French Communists have described the
movement from SMC to socialism as 'advanced democracy'.
This was to be a movement based upon a united movement of
all those exploited by the monopolies, that is, of all except the
'barons of the big trusts' — the 200 families. For the working
class, in this process, the PCF had reserved the role of

'vanguard' and progress was to be an alliance around working class interests as represented by the Communist Party.[6] No violence was done to the standard Leninist view of the party as the working class and the party as *avant garde* but the probability of alliances, the necessity even, was admitted. All this was orthodox SMC theory, part of the general Western Communist background of the 60s and something brought to the attention of the French public in the 'Champigny Manifesto' which is still referred to by the PCF as the major document of the last twenty years.[7]

Hence state monopoly capitalism is the doctrine of a Communist movement committed to an alliance strategy to arrive in power but the notion of 'advanced democracy' has been varied in recent months. Communists since the 23rd Congress of May 1979 have ceased to speak of the 'stage' in between SMC and Socialism; instead they have introduced the concept of the 'serial crisis'. It is too early to say what this means but it seems to draw out the transition over a much longer period so that at any given time it will not be possible to declare whether or not France is on the verge of a leap into Socialism, it is also much more flexible tactically as it does not commit the PCF to alliance with the Socialists and it opens up a perspective of many different kinds of battle. This last point takes up the refusal by the PCF to keep to purely parliamentary means of struggle even during the period of the common programme.[8] In a back-handed way it also makes possible collaboration with the system for Communists believe that 'reforms' (such as nationalisations) could be obtained even from right-wing governments — although it still needs Communist power to transform them into genuine advances for the working class.[9]

A number of points can be made about this theory. First it rules out revolution in the form of the traditional Leninist coup d'etat but it does not specify in what form change will come.

For example, a regression to violence is not excluded once the 'bourgeoisie' sees its interests threatened and it does not mean that concentration on parliamentary means to power should go on to the exclusion of all others. This is no mere 'parliamentary cretinism' in that demonstrations, union pressure and use of the 'parallel state', the Communist Party apparatus, is very much a part of the 'struggle for socialism'. Secondly, the prospect of wide alliances is opened out but the form is not specified. In SMC theory the Communist Party will remain the interpreter of what is the working class position on any issue and this is the PCF case.[10] Alliances around the central nucleus of the vanguard party are done on the assumption that there is only one *correct* line — that of the PCF. Thus although a broad anti-monopoly alliance of the middle classes, managers and small business is a possibility, because everybody except the tiny number of trusts is exploited, the working class is the most exploited group and most advanced and leading group. Perhaps the most important point is that, in direct contrast to 1930s Communism, it is possible to carry through piecemeal reforms hence a reformist perspective is opened out to the PCF — though exactly what is not specified.

SMC CRISIS

French Communists have been talking about the crisis of capitalism since the late 1960s just before the 'Champigny Manifesto' but that should not obscure the line of reasoning which holds that this is *the* crisis of State Monopoly Capitalism. Communists exclude the possibility that the late 1970s are witnessing a crisis caused by rising prices of primary products (nor by the late 1973 increase in petrol prices) nor is it, they say, a result of excessive wage demands by workers. For PCF spokesmen the crisis is due to an over-accumulation of capital in which the mass of appropriated profit exceeds the restricted possibilities for profitable re-investment.

Inflation, unemployment, exploitation, and slump are endemic to the SMC system. Whilst the monopolies are cutting wages and slashing costs, they cannot find purchasers for their goods because they are destroying the purchasing power upon which the market depends. However the continuing 'werewolf' greed for capital is demonstrated by the outrageous profits made by the monopolies which they invest abroad — usually in the Third World. Inflation is a result of the process of concentration in which the monopolies sell products above their real value to maintain the rate of return and they use the profit to speculate.

Thus the crisis of SMC is the crisis of the whole system and it is the crisis which marks the historical limits of the capitalist mode of production. In France the Giscardian establishment *(le pouvoir)* drained the country of the best part of its productive resources and of French work to the benefit of a handful of multi-nationals.[11] Multi-nationals export jobs, through transfer pricing they swindle the country, and by switching production around between states (or by dividing it up) they thwart national economic purposes. However this is not because the multi-nationals escape state control but because they in effect control state policies.

SMC crisis is structural and cannot be solved through modifications of the interior of the system and the solution therefore requires revolutionary steps forward. After these revolutionary reforms have been undertaken the contradiction between the increased needs of the working people and the inability of the system to satisfy these will be resolved. But this cannot be done through adaptation and the crisis extends into society and the ideology of capitalism currently prevailing.

For the French Communist Party, therefore, the SMC crisis has shown the limits of capitalism's ability to control the system through market relationships. Communists postulate the end to the post-war economic situation and believe that re-flation will not restore full employment because it will only add to the profit of the monopolies. What has been called the Keynesian 'trade-off' between stagflation and liberty no longer works for the political reason that state policy is determined by the monopolies.

Communists therefore propose a number of measures which will enable a beginning to the transformation of the SMC system. They call for a guarantee of purchasing power along with an assured increase, the development of employment, the diminution of the length of the working week, a change in the quality of life and policy around the themes of priority for the worst off, an end to austerity and a 'war' against inequalities. It is important, say the PCF, to re-animate the economy by increasing demand: this should be done by augmenting the social security benefits, by increasing the minimum wage (SMIC), and by putting up wages. However action for the lower paid will not suffice, there should also be increased expenditure by the governbment on transport, services, investment and so on. Government spending will not stimulate the economy but will begin to move the economy out of the grip of the multi-nationals creating a new social economy.[12]

Socialisation of the economy means the control of the major means of production, distribution and exchange by the workers and their allies: in a word nationalisation. Communists look to the transformation of a capitalist society into a collectivist society through these means but nationalisation is not statism because firms will have a 'democratic administration' (see below). If nationalisation of the minimum threshold is carried through this will enable the 'democratic development of a plan in accord with the interests of the workers and the nation'.[13]

With a dominant state sector prices can be set and co-ordination of economic activity undertaken according to the plan. There will be no alternative to the socialist plan because of the extent to which public sector prices can be set by act of political will, rather than in response to monopoly capitalist pressures. Small business is but the final link in a long chain reaching down from the monopolies so that they too will be integrated into socialist circuits — the same goes for farmers. This is how the state will begin 'primitive socialist accumulation' by bringing under public control the material resources of the rest of the economy. Banks, which have the power to frustrate this process, would be nationalised whilst foreign banks ought to be constrained by union committees and would lose their right to accept deposits or savings.[14]

Thus the *Communist Programme* centres on nationalisation of the minimum threshold of industries to create a new public sector which is central to PCF thinking because it allows the planning of the economy. Planning is still the PCF's one instrument despite the tendency to play this down since the great days of Stalin's five-year plans. This is why the PCF equates the extent of socialism with the extent of nationalisation but the question remains of how this can be equated with 'democratic administration'.

French Communism is still Leninist in at least one way; it equates the advance of democracy and of working class power with the Communist Party itself. For French Communists the working class equals the party or (sometimes) the CGT unions which are anyway controlled by the party. Georges Séguy and Henri Krasucki, the top CGT leaders, are members of the PCF Central Committee, 30 out of 37 Federal Secretaries are PCF and 80 out of 97 departmental secretaries are PCF. Workers would, apparently, be associated with the new state at all levels and a socialist society would be complete power for the workers — but in the PCF parlance the working class is represented by the Communist Party, they are one and the same. In the *Common Programme* the word 'democracy' is somewhat nuanced and was in the PCF reading, equated with the unions. Planning would be the work of the workers at all levels but they represented by unions and by them alone. (In the well-worn expression of the PCF the union is the transmission belt for the Party). As the CGT is under Communist sway, power for the workers under this formula spells power for the PCF.

Given this background the Communist call for democracy in the factories and workplaces takes on another meaning as does the struggle over the *Common Programme's* positions, for an elected head of each public sector — with or without split electoral colleges — would lead inexorably to PCF domination whereas Socialist nominated heads would keep Communist influence to a minimum. *'Cogestion'* by the unions is one of the principal themes of the *Common Programme* and in the case of the PCF this extends to all parts of the economy not just factories.

So the French Communist Party has been able to speak in eulogistic terms about self-management *(autogestion)* which they sternly denounced for years but without changing the content of their state-centralist vision of Socialism or of the mechanism of Communist planning.

The entire Communist programme is an alternative way to socialism. It is a non-revolutionary, peaceful (but not exclusively parliamentary) road to power but it is not a reformist road because, says the PCF, the Party will only support or enter government to carry out real changes. The brunt of Communist accusations against Social Democratic parties are that the northern Socialists have not carried through these economic changes — in particular nationalisation and planning.[15]

Footnotes

1. D. Blackmer and S. Tarrow (eds.) *Communism in Italy and France*, Princeton UP, 1975.
2. R.L. Tökés *op.cit.*, Ch.III.
3. Annie Kriegel *The French Communists*, Chicago UP 1972.
4. SMC is 'The ultimate mode of capitalist production in its imperialist stage . . . it has exhausted its historical potential', *Le Capitalisme Monopoliste d'Etat*, Paris, 1976, *Vol.II, p.440*. (Hereinafter CME). See also S.K. Holland *op.cit.*
5. 'Important productive capacities are unemployed, others are used for military ends; others, finally, are not put to use because they do not correspond to the immediate profit criteria, as for example automation and scientific research'. *CME*, Vol.II, p.425 and F.S. Kissin *op.cit.*
6. Georges Marchais *le Défi Démocratique*, Paris, ES 1972, p.71 *et. seq.* Réné Andrieu *Les communistes et la revolution*, Juillard, 1968, p.231.
7. 'Champigny Manifesto', December 5th and 6th, 1968.
8. Vide René Andrieu, *Les communistes at la revolution*, Juillard, Paris, 1968, p.241.
9. Vide, Felix Damette and Jacques Scheibling *Pour une strategie autogestionnaire*, Paris, ES, 1979, p.120ff.
10. Georges Marchais, *Parlons Franchement*, p.196.
11. Cf. *CME* Vol.I p.18 and pp.262-268. On the 'subsidy' of the private sector see H. Serge *Les Enterprises Publiques*, Paris, ES, 1975, p.148ff.
12. *l'Humanité* 29 September 1974, *et seq* and *Changer l'Economie*, P. Boccara *et alia*, ES, Paris 1977. 'The structures of society cannot adapt to current needs' first resolution of the 22nd Congress of the PCF in *Cahiers du Communisme*, Nos. 2-3, 1976, p.364 and report on the 20th Congress *ibid*, Nos. 2-3 1973, p.33.
13. E. Fajon, *l'Union c'est un combat*, p.103, *Changer de Cap*, p.16.
14. *Changer de Cap*, pp.203-204.
15. *Vide* G. Streiff *et alia*, *La Social Démocratie au Present*, Paris, ES, 1979, p.125-148 and D. Debatisse *et alia*, *Europe: La France en jeu*, Paris, ES, 1979, pp.156-171.

(This chapter was written before the 1981 elections.)

APPENDIX I

La Petite Gauche in France

by Peter Jenkins and D.S. Bell

THE UNIFIED SOCIALIST PARTY

The main components of the French Left through the 1970s were the Socialist Party and the Communist Party but this does not exhaust the number of parties or organisations (leaving aside the extreme Left). There are the Unified Socialist Party (PTU), the Left Radicals and the new Ecologists to be taken into account even though they are overshadowed by the 'big two'.

The PSU, if it is known at all to the British Left, is most likely to be associated with the events of May '68, the theme of 'autogestion', and with the political figure of Michel Rocard. Each of these images and associations offers some insight into the nature of the PSU, although an understanding of the party as such would clearly signify more than the total of these separate elements.

To start with Michael Rocard: currently a leading figure in the Socialist Party, and rival to François Mitterrand as 1981 Presidential candidate, spokesman for the 'social-democratic' wing of the PS, Rocard's positions put him on the right of the Socialist Party. His long past association with the Unified Socialist Party (member since 1960, National Secretary 1967-73, Presidential candidate 1969) clearly give him credentials of a different sort, as a radical, a man of action, which are useful when introducing him to the rank and file at public meetings, perhaps, but confusing, at best, to observers trying to plot the trajectory of his political career.

There is an element of irony here. The early PSU was similarly tied to the ambiguous and unwelcome figure of Pierre Mendes-France, who, never more than a rank and file member, abstained from taking any position of responsibility within the party. Rocard's identification with the PSU came to be more thorough, if complex. A rising civil servant, graduate of the prestigious ENA school of administration, he was groomed for leadership by Edouard Depreux, and succeeded his mentor as PSU National Secretary in 1967. Initially protected by the party name of Georges Servet, Rocard came to personify the party's main concerns, giving them a clarity and resonance which carried its influence to the 'couches nouvelles' of the new working class identified by Serge Mallet.

The characteristic themes of the PSU in the 1960s were a concern for realistic economic analysis, the strategy of the society of the socialist 'counter-plan' to the state's indicative planning, and the 'decolonising the provinces', i.e. a radical re-structuring of France's top-heavy system of government. The complementary images of the PSU and Rocard as modern, technocratic and informed were closely intertwined in the public eye.

This aspect of the PSU — as a vital, reforming agency, a 'laboratory of ideas', a 'collective intellectual', jars somewhat with its other, perhaps incompatible role, as a party of militants, a party immersed in the class struggle. This clash between the party's adopted dual roles is a consistent theme in its development, coming into sharpest relief at times of political crisis, such as the events of May-June 1968.

The PSU had been born out of the protest against the war in Algeria. In 1968, the PSU again returned to the streets in the wave of demonstrations and factory occupations unleashed by police repression of student militants. The PSU's influence in the student movement, UNEF, and its limited, but real presence on the factory floor, gave it a degree of leverage as an established political party, however small, that was denied to the myriad 'groupuscules' of the far Left. Closely identified with the student movement by the Communist Party, the PSU in turn was infected by the students' gut hostility for, and rejection of, the PCF, with serious results, such as the boycott of the latter's major demonstration of the 29th May.

Predictably, the PSU's strategy was complex, reflecting its dual role as party of protest, and party of radical reform. On the one hand, the party's aim was to co-ordinate and develop the as then limited and sectarian 'action committees' as prototype organs of dual power, as in Nantes. On the other hand, it was to promote a parliamentary resolution to the current stage of the crisis, with the election of a coalition government acceptable to the socialist FGDS, and the PCF, under the leadership of Pierre Mendes-France. The PCF's hostility to the scheme effectively torpedoed it, and the rally at Charlety stadium, intended as opening a further round of *electoral* struggle, became, instead, the high-water mark of the May events.

The PSU's political line during this rapidly changing period seems clear only in retrospect. Many militants, confused at the time, opted for active involvement in local struggles. Rocard's own leadership role is hard to identify, and was perhaps less positive than that of other leadership cadres such as Yvain Craipeau, working with the action committees.

The immediate legacy of 1968 for the PSU was, like all the organisations of the Left, an influx of members, taking it from the 1967 level of 11,599 to 15,511 a year later.[1] With this came an established influence in the student movement, and, to a smaller extent, in the labour movement, particularly in the CFDT. Turning away from its former technocratic concerns, the PSU redefined itself as a revolutionary party, with close and developing links with the far Left. Rocard, as the public face of the party, and its relatively successful Presidential candidate in 1969, made the necessary verbal accommodations, and moved to the Left with his party of impatient, youthful revolutionaries.

In retrospect, Rocard appears to have ridden out the revolutionary wave which surged through and out of the PSU, taking many members with it. By 1971, the PSU had broken with its post-1968 project of regrouping the far Left. Its focus was now on the subversive potential contained in the concept of 'autogestion', or self-management, partially realised in the Yugoslav experiments, briefly revived in the 1968 factory occupations, now to be applied to industry, local government and all levels of society. Or, as one PSU militant put it, "People don't give a damn about Marx, Trotsky or Mao. All they are looking for is a solution to their problems and the meaninglessness of their lives. That's what we hope autogestion can be for them".[2]

Autogestion was to become the party's key contribution to the political debates of the 1970s, as the Union of the Left between a revived Socialist Party and the PCF discussed their probable electoral victory in 1978. Reform at the top, argued the PSU, was meaningless without a corresponding change in the power of working people to control their own lives in the factory, in the school, and in the community.

The close association of the PSU with the theme of autogestion has outlasted the bitter trauma of Rocard's defection to the Socialist Party in 1974, with a thousand or so supporters. Certainly, the party lost in Rocard an able, urbane and articulate spokesman, with an establshed national political reputation. Yet, paradoxically, it may also have gained in the sense that, with its leading figure gone, the party has still survived, albeit at a cost measured in terms of lower electoral returns and reduced media interest.

Rocard's defection acted as a focus which sharply defined the political limitations and weaknesses of the party. Essentially, these concern the party's attitude towards social democracy. The PSU originally developed out of the decay of the old SFIO, but did not break with it on a broad political basis, but rather on the *specific* themes of opposition to the war in Algeria, and of resistance to the Fifth Republic established by de Gaulle. For certain periods, the PSU has emerged as the political expression of the non-communist Left, and, almost, as the radical, uncompromising wing of social democracy. Yet the re-emergence of social democracy onto the political scene, as with Mitterrand's election campaign of 1965, and more importantly, the rapid development of the Socialist Party since 1971, led on both occassions to the danger of the PSU being recouped by a form of social democracy which had regained its dynamism, support and credibility. Significantly, both moves by the PSU leadership to make an accommodation with social democracy, in 1967 and again in 1974, were vigorously rejected by a vigilant PSU rank and file (led by Rocard on the first occasion, if not on the second).

The danger of recoupment has never been likely with the PCF, nor, despite the experiences of 1968-71, with the far Left. This, it can be argued, indicates the existence of an organic link between the PSU and social democracy, which, in effect, occupy the same political terrain. The PSU's fortunes are rising only when social democracy is demoralised and fragmented, and decline when the latter is once again a serious force.

At certain key times, the PSU has indeed displayed a tendency to defer to the project of social democracy, as in 1974, when the party chose to support Mitterrand, rather than run Charles Piaget, the Lip strike leader, as Presidential candidate for the 'mouvement autogestionnaire'. Again, following the disappointing results in the Presidential election (1.1 per cent), and the legislative elections (1.93 per cent) of 1981, where the party's electoral marginalisation continued apace, the PSU seems to have opted for the role of 'radical conscience' of the Socialist government, rather than adopting a position of 'contestation'. The party's internal tensions over this attitude are clear from the differences between the 'advisers' and the 'activist' tendency at its most recent congress. The original ambiguities inherent in the founding of the PSU in 1960 are still evident two decades later.[3]

Despite these real weaknesses, it must be acknowledged that the PSU has survived as an organised political force, albeit with a membership now reduced to 5,500.[4] It has twice rejected the social democratic temptation, avoided becoming a PCF satellite, and warded off the recruiting raids of the far Left. Its current concerns are now less exclusively industrial, and embrace questions affecting the environment, nuclear power, and the oppression of women. The PSU's thousand or so local councillors give it a small footing in local politics, which in turn requires a degree of recognition and co-operation from the Socialist, Communist and Ecology parties. Doggedly federal in terms of organisation, the party has an enviable and highly democratic internal structure. Writing an epitaph for the PSU is no doubt a premature enterprise (it has been tried many times in the past!), but any serious appreciation of its role would have to recognise its imagination and continuing tenacity in bringing crucial issues — nuclear power, feminism, autogestion — forcefully to the attention of the wider labour movement.

References
1.   Charles Hauss, *The New Left in France: the Unified Socialist Party,* Greenwood Press, Conn., USA, 1978, p.215.
2.   *Ibid.,* p.200.
3.   Vladimir Claude Fisera and Peter Jenkins, "The Unified Socialist Party (PSU) since 1968", in David Bell, (ed.), *Contemporary French Political Parties,* Groom Helm, 1982.
4.   *Tribune Socialiste Hebdo,* No.907, 6-12 Janvier 1982, p.7.

THE LEFT RADICALS (MRG)

The Radical Party is the oldest political party in France and finds its origins in the Third Republic of which it was the dominant grouping. As a pivotal centre group it played an influential role in the Fourth Republic but the Fifth Republic has seen a clear decline in its influence and a split into the Left wing then led by Maurice Faure and a Right wing led by Servan-Schreiber.

Maurice Faure's wing of the Radical party formed the *Mouvement des Radicaux de Gauche* (MRG) in 1973 and has since fought the elections of 1973 and 1978 with the Socialists under the title of UGSD *(Union de la Gauche Socialiste et Démocrate)* which enables the two to avoid direct electoral competition. MRG, or Left Radicals, supported the common programme of the Left which the rest of the party found too Socialist and Left-wing to swallow, but its position is a difficult one because it is small and tends to be a mere puppet of the Socialists. Most Radical influence has been directed to bargaining with the Socialists over Assembly seats and city council positions with a continuing concern to 'moderate' the common programme whose measures for nationalisation have always been difficult for the MRG to swallow.

Also, because it is a marginal formation, the MRG Left Radicals have been subject to erosion by the Right and some of their members have changed camp. Yet, it is precisely this hinge position that gives the MRG its influence. Left Radicals are needed to entice centre votes into the Left camp and their allotment of ministries and seats is for that reason higher than their electoral position would lead the observer to expect. In fact the MRG has attracted a number of ambitious people and has launched some new ideas. Typical of the latter is their new leader the Deputy Mayor of La Rochelle Michel Crépeau who espoused ecological ideas before their time and made his city into an ecological experimental zone and who was their 1981 presidential candidate.

The other major figure of the Radical Left was Robert Fabre who was responsible for precipitating the crisis in the union of the Left in the autumn of 1977 when he refused to accept the renegotiation proposals on nationalisation. But the Left Radical position was too weak and too dependent on the success of Left union to permit such strong-arm tactics and Fabre lost the leadership of the Left Radicals to Crépeau under a hail of criticism.

Left Radicals are a small group, mainly notables, but they are important in marginal constituencies which the Left must win to take power. They have not succeeded in imposing their own stamp on politics and even the mid-1980 attempt to float a possible presidential candidature (from Crépeau) fell flat particularly since many interpreted it as another way of forcing Michel Rocard onto the Socialists. But the MRG candidate was important in a presidential campaign because his two per cent came from the Socialists and possibly took enough to deprive Mitterrand of the lead on the first ballot.

Left Radicals are somewhat directionless but remain close to the Socialists and will remain important in their role of attracting floating voters.

ECOLOGISTS

In France the ecologists, although small, are not unimportant and are a phenomenon of the late 1970s starting with their patchy entry into the municipal elections of 1977 and ecologists managed to pull some 2.14 per cent at the 1977 European elections. There has been a tendency to assume that the ecologists take votes from the Left (and in particular the PS) but they have done damage to the Right (mainly south of the Loire). Ecologists are well represented in Paris and in the provinces though their electorate is mainly a white collar middle class worried about damage to the environment, unplanned city growth and nuclear power. Brice Lalonde the ecology candidate in the election of 1981 probably damaged Giscard more than any other candidate. In 1974 the ecologist candidate René Dumont was a well-respected academic who called on his voters to support François Mitterrand at the second ballot.

Appendix II
Statistics of the French Left 1958-1981

	Oct 1958		Nov 1962		Presidential 1965	March 1967		June 1968		Presidential 1969	March 1973		Presidential 1974	March 1978		Presidential 1981	June 1981	
	% of vote	seats	% of vote	seats		% of vote	seats	% of vote	seats		% of vote	seats		% of vote	seats		% of vote	seats
PCF	19.2	10	21.7	41		22.5		20	34	Duclos 21.5%	21.4	73		20.8	86	15.3%	16.17	44
Socialists SFIO/PS[NB]	15.7	44	12.5	66	Mitterrand 32.2%§	19		16.5	116	Defferre 5.1%	20.8	88	Mitterrand 43.3%†	22.59	104	Mitterrand 25.8%*	37.51	269
Radicals/ MRG	8.3	32	7.8	39								12		2.11	10	2.2%	N.A.	14
PSU			2.4	0		2.1	4	4	4	Rocard 3.7	3.3	1				1.1%	0.7	—

(All results are for the first ballot)

§1965 — 45.5% on the 2nd ballot. †1974 — 49.3% on the 2nd ballot. *1981 — 51.75% on the 2nd ballot.

N.B. After 1962 the Socialists and Left Radicals had apparently decided not to compete and are therefore put together.

APPENDIX III

The Second Pierre Mauroy Government (June 1981)

Prime Minister: Pierre Mauroy.

Ministers of State
Interior and Decentralisation: Gaston Defferre.
External Trade: Michel Jobert (Democratic Movement ex-Gaullist).
Transport: Charles Fiterman (PCF).
Plan: Michel Rocard.
Research and Technology: J-P Chevènement.

Minister
National Solidarity: Nicole Questiaux.

Ministers — Délégués auprés du P.M.
Womens' Rights: Yvette Roudy.
Relations with Parliament: André Labarrère.
Civil Service and Administrative Reform: Anicet Le Pors (PCF).

Ministers and Delegate Ministers
Minister of Justice: Robert Badinter.
Foreign Affairs: Claude Cheysson.
Delegate to Foreign Affairs for Europe: André Chandernagor.
Delegate to Foreign Affiars for Co-operation and Development: J-P Cot.
Defence: Charles Hernu.
Economics and Finance: Jacques Delors.
Delegate to Economics and Finance for the Budget: Laurent Fabius.
Education: Alain Savary.
Agriculture: Edith Cresson.
Industry: Pierre Drayfus.
Delegate to Industry for Energy: Edmond Hervé.
Commerce and Small Business: André Delilis.
Culture: Jack Lang.
Labour: Jean Auroux.
Health: Jack Ralite (PCF).
Leisure/Free Time: André Henry.
Delegate to Leisure/Free Time for Youth and Sports: Edwige Avice.
Housing and Cities: Roger Quillot.
Environment: Michel Crépeau (Left Radicals).
Marine: Louis Le Pensec.
Communication: Georges Filloud.

Former Soldiers: Jean Laurian.
Consumer Minister: Catherine Lalumière.
Professional Training: Marcel Rigout (PCF).

Secretaries of State to the Prime Minister
Extension of the Public Sector: Jean Le Garrec.
Repatriates: Raymond Courrière.

Secretaries of State to Individual Ministers
Overseas France (Ministry of the Interior): Henri Emmanuelli.
Family (Solidarity): Georgina Dufoix.
Old People (Solidarity): Joseph Franchesi.
Immigrants (Solidarity): François Autain.
(Defence): Georges Lemoine.
(Agriculture): André Cellard.
Tourism (Leisure/Free Time): François Abadie.

(All Ministers are Socialist except where indicated and the list is in order of seniority).

BIBLIOGRAPHY OF ENGLISH SOURCES

Up-to-date material on the French parties of the Left is not all that abundant in English. However the Byron Criddle article on "The French Part: Socialiste" in W. Paterson/A.H. Thomas (eds) *Social Democratic Parties in Western Europe* (Croom Helm) 1977, is probably the best inroduction and there are also the two articles by Vincent Wright and Howard Machin "The French Socialist Party: Success and the Problems of Success" in *Political Quarterly* January 1975 pages 36-52, and "The French Socialist Party in 1973: Performance and Prospects" in *Government and Opposition,* Spring 1974 pages 123-145. John Frears *Political Parties and Elections in The French Fifth Republic* (Charles Hurst) 1977, contains an excellent discussion of the Left as does Vincent Wright's *The Government and Politics of France* (Hutchinson) 1978 and the Left under the Fourth Republic is discussed in Philip William's *Crisis and Compromise* (Longman) 1972 and recently (but before the 1981 elections) there has been R.W. Johnson's *The Long March of the French Left* (Macmillan) 1980.

Interest in Eurocommunism has meant that a variety of publications contain new material on the Communist Party in France. Books on the subject include Annie Kriegel's *The French Communists* (Chicago UP) 1972, R. Tiersky's *French Communism 1920-1972* (Columbia UP) 1974 and D. Blackmer/S. Tarrow (eds) *Communism in Italy and France* (Princeton UP) 1975, but these were all written before the Eurocommunist phenomenon got into full swing. For an appreciation of the relationship of French Communism to Eurocommunism there is a Labour Party pamphlet on the subject *The Dilemma of Eurocommunism* and the 1979 Penguin edited by Edward Mortimer *et alia, Eurocommunism,* plus the substantial (expensive) R.L. Tökés (ed) *Eurocommunism and Détente* (New York UP) 1979 (Chapter three) and F. Claudin's discussion of Eurocommunism called *Eurocommunism* (NLB) 1979.

On relations between the Socialists and Communists see John Frears, *Political Parties and Electrions in the French Fifth Republic* and Ian Campbell "The French Communists and the Union of the Left" in *Parliamentary Affairs,* Summer 1976, pages 246-263. For the Socialist Party in the 1960s see F.L. Wilson's *The French Democratic Left 1963-1969* (Stanford UP) 1971. There is also a translation of the now defunct *Common Programme* (translated by J. Greenwood *et alia)* by Southampton UP — this is not discussed at length here.

ABBREVIATIONS

CERES   Centre D'Etudes de Récherches et d'Education Socialistes.
CFDT   Confédération Française Démocratique du Travail.
CGT   Confédération Générale du Travail.
CIR   Convention des Institutions Républicains.
CNPF   Conseil National du Patronat Français.
CRS   Compagnies Républicaines de Sécurité.
DOM   Départments d'Outre-Mer.

FEN   Fédération de l'Education Nationale.
FO   Force Ouvrière.
HLM   Habitations à Loyer Modéré.
MRG   Mouvement des Radicaux de Gauche.
MRP   Mouvement Républicain Populaire.
PCF   Parti Communiste Français.
PS   Parti Socialiste.
PSU   Parti Socialiste Unifié.
RI   Républicains Indépendants.
RPR   Rassemblement pour la République.
SFIO   Section Française de l'Internationale Ouvrière.
UDF   Union pour la Démocratie Française.
UDSR   Union Démocratique et Socialiste de la Résistance.
UGDS   Union de la Gauche Socialiste et Démocrate.

NOTES ON CONTRIBUTORS

D.S. Bell is a lecturer in Politics at the University of Leeds. David Hanley is a lecturer in Modern French History and Politics at the University of Reading where he is a member of the Department of French Studies. He is currently researching the contemporary theoretical debates within the French Left and is one of the joint authors of *Contemporary France: Politics and Society since 1945*. Eric Shaw is a lecturer in Politics at Manchester Polytechnic and formerly worked in the International Department of the Labour Party. In addition to being a member of the Labour Party's Western Europe Sub-Committee Eric Shaw is one of the co-authors of the Labour Party pamphlet *The Dilemma of Eurocommunism*.

The Nuclear Era

Professor Jacobsen draws on his background as historian, Sovietologist and strategic analyst in this broad examination of the 'nuclear era'. He combines a concise history of the evolution of the superpowers 'balance' and the emergence of lesser nuclear powers with a vigorous challenge to reigning strategic doctrines and the premises upon which they are based.

The author's perspective transcends the narrow sectarianism that has dominated (and side-tracked) defence debates of recent years and calls for an end to the dialogue of the deaf that has resulted. His unique combination of historical analysis with in-depth discussion of the views of strategists, arms controllers and disarmament advocates, and his focus on the intertwined military-political, scientific-technological and developmental trends of the '80s give this book rare value both for reference and as a powerful contribution to the current debate.

156pp   Cloth £14.50   ISBN 0 85124 346 0
Demy 8vo   Paper £3.95   ISBN 0 85124 347 9

Spokesman University Paperback No.35

Spokesman University Paperbacks

Out of print in paperback. Clothbound editions still available.

SPOKESMAN, Bertrand Russell House, Gamble Street, Nottingham, NG7 4ET. Tel: 0602 708318.

Out of Crisis:
A Project for European Recovery

Edited by Stuart Holland

This report projects an 'Alternative Economic Strategy' which goes beyond either Britain or the EEC alone to a genuine alternative strategy for Europe and the international economy.

Developing the seminal debate begun in *New Socialist* by Stuart Holland, Francis Cripps and others, this report combines the ideas of political economists, politicians and trade unionists from over a dozen countries. The report challenges monetarism and the slump syndrome with a new model of development for the West European economies. Focusing on strategic aims — to reflate, restructure, and redistribute resources — it also shows the convergence between policies of the main parties of the European Left on public spending, planning and economic democracy.

This will be one of the most important publications of the year.

150pp approx. Paper £2.95 *ISBN 0 85124 354 1*
Spokesman University Paperback No.39
European Socialist thought No.11

Bevanism:
Labour's High Tide

by Mark Jenkins

This is a closely researched and much praised piece of contemporary history. First published as a hardback in 1979, it is based almost entirely on original source material.

"Students of the post-1945 Labour movement have urgently needed a detailed analysis of the components of Bevanism, to set alongside Philip Williams masterly biography of Hugh Gaitskell. This vigorous and highly stimulating book by Mark Jenkins makes an excellent start." Times Literary Supplement.

"Bevanism is an exceedingly well researched, thoughtful and important book. Nobody who counts himself or herself part of the Left can afford to ignore it." Royden Harrison, Marxism Today.

360pp Dmy 8vo
Spokesman
University Paperback No.33

Cloth £18   0 85124 273 1

Paper £4.95   0 85124 322 3